SILVER GOLDFISH

LOUD & CLEAR: THE 10 KEYS TO DELIVERING MEMORABLE BUSINESS PRESENTATIONS

Stan Phelps and Alan Hoffler

Published by 9 INCH Marketing

Editing by Lee Heinrich of Write Way Publishing
Layout by Amit Dey
Cover design by Joshua Vaughan

ISBN: 978-1-952234-04-0

First Printing: 2020
Printed in the United States of America

Copies of *Silver Goldfish* are available for bulk orders. For further details and special pricing, please e-mail: stan@purplegoldfish.com or call +1.919.360.4702.

DEDICATION

This book is dedicated to my late dad, John Phelps. His nickname was the "Silver Fox." As a proud member of the US Signal Corps, he reinforced the importance for me to always come across as loud and clear.

— Stan Phelps

I dedicate this work to my dad, Wyck Hoffler, a true master of words (and just about everything else).

— Alan Hoffler

ACKNOWLEDGMENTS

We'd like to thank everyone who inspired us, supported us, or provided feedback and examples for the book:

Jay Baer, Jeff Bailey, Laura Bergells, Rob Biesenbach, Barry Borgerson, Joseph Campbell, David Cervi, Stephen Covey Jr, Dave Crenshaw, Chris Croft, Todd Dewett, Hermann Ebbinghaus, Bryan Eisenberg, Justin Jones-Fosu, Greg Ferguson, Carmine Gallo, Robert Gaskins, Andrew Gilman, Seth Godin, Christopher Guest, John D. Hanson, Kim Harrison, Chip Heath, Dan Heath, Danielle Hennis, Jason Hewlett, Chris Malone, Kathy McAfee, Dr. John Medina, Albert Mehrabian, Donald Miller, Nick Morgan, Edward Murphy, Jeff Nischwitz, Jennifer Pacilan, John Phelps Sr, Marcey Rader, David Rendall, Patsy Rodenburg, Vincent Schmidt, Milo Shapiro, Ewan Spence, Stephanie Scotti, Lyndsie Selwyn, Bill Stainton, Harold Stolovitch, Kevin Synder, Eddie Van Halen, Viveka von Rosen, Jeff Toister, Waldo Waldman, and Leesa Wallace

TABLE OF CONTENTS

INTRODUCTION

by
Stan Phelps

*"There are only two types of speakers in this world.
The nervous . . . and the liars."*

-Mark Twain

What's the most common fear for humans? It's speaking. According to *Forbes*, "The fear of public speaking is the most common fear and prevents many people from achieving their potential."[1] A shocking 74 percent of Americans have fears and anxiety toward public speaking.[2]

Our number two fear—dying.

Does this make any sense? We, as humans, have so lost perspective that when asked what we fear the most, we will choose a threat to our identity over actual death! In the brilliant words of comedian Jerry Seinfeld, "For the average person, if you have to be at a funeral, you would rather be in the casket than doing the eulogy."

The fear of speaking and presenting is called glossophobia. Some may feel a slight nervousness at the thought of public speaking, while others experience full-on panic and fear.[3]

---

1. https://www.forbes.com/sites/work-in-progress/2012/10/09/five-reasons-why-the-fear-of-public-speaking-is-great-for-you/#10154caf3b82
2. https://brandongaille.com/14-fear-public-speaking-statistics/
3. https://www.psycom.net/glossophobia-fear-of-public-speaking

Why? Because our brain has a hard time distinguishing between actual risk (loss of life) and perceived risk (threat to our identity). Our brains are wired to respond to threat in a particular way—regardless of the actual threat.

To my knowledge, no one has literally died giving a presentation. But think about what happens when you stand up or sit down to present. Your brain goes into threat mode. Your amygdala senses a threat and sends signals to your limbic system. The limbic system effectively shuts down your neocortex, the thinking part of your brain. It then releases chemicals that increase your heart rate, breathing rate, and sweat gland activity.

And to be candid, even for an experienced presenter, these feelings of nervousness and excitement never completely go away. You can't unwire or unlearn biology. Mark Twain made light of this when he said, "There are only two types of speakers in this world. The nervous . . . and the liars."

Overcoming these feelings and becoming great at presenting/speaking is the focus of *Silver Goldfish* with co-author Alan Hoffler. Alan Hoffler is a self-proclaimed philorator. What's that? It's Greek for a "teacher and lover of speaking." (Well, it's actually made up, but if you ask Alan, he'd tell you that the root words are valid. Or at least his friend who took a semester of Greek said they were.) We've put our heads together to share what we've collectively learned about creating memorable business presentations. Those lessons have been honed from our collective thousands of hours on the stage and watching/learning from others on the stage. We're going to give you numerous tips to improve your presenting skills and your ability to craft your message. Valuable tips. Tips that will change the way you prepare and the way you perform. Tips that will change the reaction of your audience and the results you see.

RETHINKING TIPS

While the precise origin of the word TIP is uncertain, it is commonly traced to coffeehouses in seventeenth century England. The word "tips" was first used for gratuities. A jar with a sign reading, "To Insure Prompt Service" sat on the counter. You put a coin in the jar to be served quickly.[4] We're going to adopt a different acronym for the word:

TO

IMPROVE

PRESENTATION

SKILLS

Silver Goldfish will share tips on how to be heard "Loud" and "Clear" when presenting.

You are in good hands reading this book. My co-author Alan Hoffler has trained thousands of people to become effective and engaging presenters. Including me. He's my speaking coach.

MEETING ALAN

I moved from Norwalk, Connecticut, to Cary, North Carolina, in the summer of 2012. My first book, *Purple Goldfish - How to Win Customers and Influence Word of Mouth*, had been published earlier that year. My goal was to become a full-time author and speaker. As a marketer and someone new to the area, I began to attend the monthly luncheons for the Triangle AMA (American Marketing

---

4. https://www.thespruceeats.com/evolution-of-the-coffee-house-765825

Association). When I saw the December topic, my interest was piqued:

> **December 20** – Triangle AMA December Luncheon – **Championship Speaking,** 11:30 a.m.-1:15 p.m. at Brier Creek Country Club in Raleigh. In this fast-paced and example-filled session, Alan Hoffler (@alanhoffler), Public Speaking Coach at MillsWyck Communications, will share three critical components to make every message memorable with your audience. Cost: $30 for members, $40 for nonmembers

I immediately purchased my ticket for "Championship Speaking." Two days before the luncheon I contracted the flu. When the luncheon date arrived, my spirit was still willing, but my body was weak. I reluctantly had to miss it. A few days later I reached out to Alan via email and asked for a meeting. He agreed and we met at a local coffee shop in Cary. A friendship was born. I would subsequently join BORN, an advanced Toastmasters Group that meets weekly. Alan had been one of the early members of BORN and helped shape its culture and format. It is a place where you can try out new material, watch great speakers, and hone your skills as a presenter.

It was at BORN that I began my journey as a Professional Speaker. Part of my training in 2013 was a two-day course that Alan hosted called **Powerful, Persuasive Speaking**. Alan still hosts these workshops four or five times a year and conducts workshops for companies whenever they have a need. My education was in full-swing. I began to collect tips and techniques. In July of 2014, I published a Slideshare called "21 Rules to Help You Rock Your Next Presentation."[5] It has since been viewed over 60,000 times and downloaded nearly 2,000 times on Slideshare.

---

5. https://www.slideshare.net/9INCHMARKETING/21-rules-to-help-you-rock-your-next-presentation

In 2015, I was awarded a spot at TEDx Douglasville. Once notified, I immediately connected with Alan. He guided and coached me through my talk, "Rethinking Business with the Power of G.L.U.E." I was now a full-time author and speaker and giving up to 85 presentations per year.

In 2019, I earned my CSP® (Certified Speaking Professional)™ from the National Speakers Association. It is the highest earned international designation reserved for the top echelon of professional speakers. The designation is based on experience (over 250 paid speaking engagements), income level, educational requirements, and client/peer review. This was also the year I asked Alan about his interest in teaming up to write *Silver Goldfish*. I'm excited that the book has come to life.

Let me give you a little background on how the book is set-up. *Silver Goldfish* is divided into four parts.

The first section is "The Why." We make the case for why you should invest in becoming a more engaging and memorable presenter. Here we'll tackle the biggest myth in communication and explain the meaning behind the Silver Goldfish. We'll delve into the meaning of "five by five" and silver. We'll explore the idea that little things can make a huge difference in the metaphor of a goldfish. We'll also shed the notion of a silver bullet in communication.

The second section is "The What." Here we explore the keys to coming across "Loud" and "Clear" when you present. Specifically, we'll address how to rise above distractions with your presentation skills. You'll learn tips on how to impress, connect, express, facilitate, and entertain your audience. In addition, you'll understand how to craft your content with clarity and organize your presentation in a way that makes your message memorable.

The third section is "The How." Here we'll share the six step S.I.L.V.E.R. process for creating a presentation. The first three letters involve preparation: Starting, Illustrating, and Learning. The second three provide guidance for the actual delivery of your presentation: Vaulting, Educating, and Requesting.

The last section of the book gives you the Five Key Takeaways.

Ready to jump in and explore the biggest myth of communication?

STAND OUT IN A SEA OF SAMENESS (THE WHY)

CHAPTER 1

MYTH OF COMMUNICATION

"The single biggest problem in communication is the illusion that it has taken place."

— (attributed to) George Bernard Shaw

You just finished a business presentation. Perhaps it was a sales pitch, a conference presentation, or a divisional update. People nodded as you finished. Some may have come up and congratulated you on the pitch, update, or talk, so you're feeling good. You're convinced you did a good job communicating your message and you're ready to see what big thing happens next you.

But let's assess the situation. How can you we tell if the desired communication has taken place? You can do so by answering these three questions:

1. Can your audience recall the central message, your One Thing?
2. Are they able to apply the message to their lives?
3. Did they understand the call to action and know what to do next?

Here's the probable reality. If you are like most presenters, you likely missed the mark.

You bought into the myth. In the words of George Bernard Shaw, "The single biggest problem in communication is the illusion that it has taken place."

The fact that you might be an ineffective presenter is most likely not your fault. You probably are emulating the hundreds, if not thousands, of presentations you've seen. You may have also heard some bad advice for presenting.

SELF-LIMITING BELIEFS

We act according to what we believe, whether or not it is true. These beliefs may be limiting us. That causes a world of problems for presenters, because there are some crazy beliefs out there:

- You should stand with your arms crossed. (Or never cross your arms.)

- Never put your hands in your pockets. (Or hands in your pockets will make you look relaxed.)

- Open with a joke. (Or never use jokes.)

- Tell 'em what you're gonna tell 'em. Tell 'em. Tell 'em what you told 'em.

- Look at spots on the wall behind your audience. (Next stop, optometrist—I'm seeing spots.)

- Imagine your audience naked. (Must be different audiences than we usually get.)

- Be you. (As though you had another option.)

Whether or not those things are true, if you BELIEVE they are true, they will affect your behavior, and they may cause you to end up looking unprofessional or losing the respect of your audience. In the business world, you may also lose clients, revenue, opportunity, and credibility.

When it comes to presenting, your behavior matters. Your behavior determines whether your audience is bored or floored; elated or deflated; engaged or feeling aged. You have the power, through your preparation and on-stage behavior, to affect change in the life and actions of your audience. It's a huge responsibility and undertaking. It's a still larger opportunity.

Whether you are in sales, applying for a job, the breakout session speaker at a conference, leading a meeting, or the voice on the webinar, both what and how you communicate will determine the outcome for your audience. You cannot assume they follow your logic or understand what you intend for them to receive. They are different from you.

In Alan's house, there are frequent discussions about whether or not a particular piece of information was transmitted. "You never told me that." "Yes, I did, yesterday afternoon." "No, you didn't. You told me about A, but not about B." "Well, I'm sure I did. You didn't listen."

Any of those accusations may be correct, but who is right doesn't matter. What does matter is that the desired communication did not take place. It all hinges on your definition of communication. We like to ask: "What's your definition of success in communication?" The answers are usually something like, "I get the job," "We make the sale/get the contract," or "My child obeys." But those aren't communication successes. They are interview, sales, and parenting successes. So the question gets asked again, "What's your definition of COMMUNICATION success?" It's difficult to nail down. Here's a simple definition we've settled on:

> Communication occurs when the AUDIENCE can repeat your message in their language.

What they choose to do with your message is out of your control. Oh sure, you can manipulate, persuade, and guilt people into actions some of the time. But ultimately, the only thing you can control is the voice and clarity of your message. You can maximize the chance that it hits the right place in your audience's mind at the right time and in the right way. That's all you can control. Be "Loud" and be "Clear."

Unfortunately, every day millions of people lead boring meetings or miss the chance to impress a unique audience assembled to hear them speak. It's a precious few who excel at communicating effectively. Many executives are some of the worst communicators around. They lead town halls, executive retreats, and one-on-ones, ending with such jewels as, "Well, I hope you found this helpful today." or "That's about all I've got. Any questions?"

We've never met a person in the corporate world who wanted more meetings, more PowerPoint to consume, or more emails from their boss. They do want clarity. They want to be able to understand without guessing or having to search for the hidden meaning. They want actionable directives that get results.

GOAL OF COMMUNICATION

We're not playing word search games in our communications. We're trying to drive a business and a career forward and to impart specific information with a measurable goal or action in mind.

Perhaps we should start by asking what we want to accomplish. Then we can figure out how this presentation thing works. And finally we can train ourselves to mimic the good and be done with the bad.

Harold Stoltovich shared an important lesson with the title of his excellent business training book, *Telling Ain't Training.* Just because you "went over the slides" does not mean the audience understood, cared, or will do anything as a result of your presentation. Finishing is not the measure of success.

The people who can tell you if communication happened are the most important people in the room: your audience. Right now, they're not here to ask. So let's figure out some little things that will make a constructive difference in your presentations. We call them Silver Goldfish. Why Silver?

CHAPTER 2

WHY SILVER?

"Every crowd has a silver lining."

— P.T. Barnum

*S*ilver Goldfish is the tenth color in the Goldfish series. It follows *Purple* (Customer Experience), *Green* (Employee Engagement), *Golden* (Loyalty), *Blue* (Technology), *Red* (Purpose), *Pink* (Brand Strategy/Differentiation), *Yellow* (Happiness), *Gray* (Leadership/Generational Insights), and Diamond (Sales/ Client Management). Why Silver and why a Goldfish? Let's start with silver and a little background on the use of colors.

The colors in the initial trilogy of books were an ode to an iconic American city and its most famous event. That city is New Orleans. Purple, green, and gold are the three official colors of Mardi Gras. It's a reference to New Orleans because there is one word from Louisiana that exemplifies the concept of doing a little something extra. That word is lagniappe. Pronounced lan-yap, it is a Creole word (mix of French and Spanish) meaning an "added gift" or "to give more." The practice originated in Louisiana in the 1840s whereby a merchant would give a customer a little something extra at the time of purchase. It is a signature personal touch by the business that creates goodwill and promotes word of mouth.

According to Webster's:

> **LAGNIAPPE** (lanˈyəəp, lăn-yăpˈ) *Chiefly Southern Louisiana & Mississippi*
>
> 1. A small gift presented by a store owner to a customer with the customer's purchase.
>
> 2. An extra or unexpected gift or benefit. Also called boot.

Mark Twain was smitten with the word when he moved to the Crescent City. He wrote about lagniappe in the book *Life on the Mississippi*:

> We picked up one excellent word—a word worth traveling to New Orleans to get; a nice limber, expressive,

handy word—"lagniappe." They pronounce it lanny-yap. It is Spanish—so they said. We discovered it at the head of a column of odds and ends in the Picayune [newspaper] the first day; heard twenty people use it the second; inquired what it meant the third; adopted it and got facility in swinging it the fourth. It has a restricted meaning, but I think the people spread it out a little when they choose. It is the equivalent of the thirteenth roll in a baker's dozen. It is something thrown in, gratis, for good measure. The custom originated in the Spanish quarter of the city.

In the trilogy, *Purple Goldfish* focused on the little things you could do to improve the customer experience, *Green Goldfish* examined how to drive engagement to improve the employee experience, and the third book, *Golden Goldfish,* uncovered the importance of your "vital few" in business. Specifically, how do you do the little things to take care of your best customers/employees.

The fourth book, *Blue Goldfish,* (co-authored with Evan Carroll) revealed how to leverage technology, data, and analytics to improve the customer experience. Blue was a reference to a tenth century Danish king named Harald Gormsson. Gormsson united Scandinavia and converted the Danes to Christianity. His nickname was Bluetooth, a reference to his dead tooth that had turned blue over time. In the 1990s, Bluetooth became the codename for the wireless area networking standard created by IBM, Ericsson, Nokia, and Cisco. Blue highlights convergence, just as Bluetooth was the result of a consortium and how King Harald united Scandinavia. Blue represents the convergence of big data and little data coming together to deliver high-level personalized experiences.

In the fifth color, *Red Goldfish* (co-authored with Graeme Newell) explored how being "for purpose" drives happiness and adds a sense of meaning for customers, employees, and society. Red was inspired by the lead singer of the band U2 and the RED Campaign launched in 2006.

In the sixth color, *Pink Goldfish* (co-authored with David Rendall) returned to the marketing roots of Purple. It examined differentiation and how to create competitive separation in business. Pink was inspired by David wearing head-to-toe pink both on and off stage.

The seventh color was Yellow. *Yellow Goldfish* (co-authored with Rosaria Cirillo Louwman) looked at how companies can do a little extra to contribute to the happiness of its customers, employees, and society. Yellow was inspired by the warmth of the sun and the yellow, smiling, happy face created by Harvey Ball in 1963 for a State Mutual Life Insurance advertisement.

The eighth color was Gray. *Gray Goldfish* (co-authored with Brian Doyle) examined how to navigate the gray areas of leading five different generations in the workforce: Matures, Boomers, Generation X, Millennials, and GenZ. It is no longer a "one-size-fits-all" leadership proposition.

The ninth color was literally a gem. The *Diamond Goldfish* (co-authored with Travis Carson and Tony Cooper) was about sales and client management. It explored how to excel under pressure and operate via the Diamond Rule in business. The use of Diamond was inspired by how the gem is created. To quote Henry Kissinger, "*A diamond is a chunk of coal that did well under pressure.*"

That brings us to silver. There are three reasons for the second metal in the series. They are readability, conductivity, and polishability. Let's examine each.

READABILITY

Readability was inspired by Stan's late father. Nicknamed the "Silver Fox," John Phelps Sr. enlisted in the United States Army Air Force at the age of 17. After finishing basic training in early 1948, he was sent to school in Fort Monmouth, New Jersey, to become a member of the United States Signal Corps. Here is his ID card from the school:

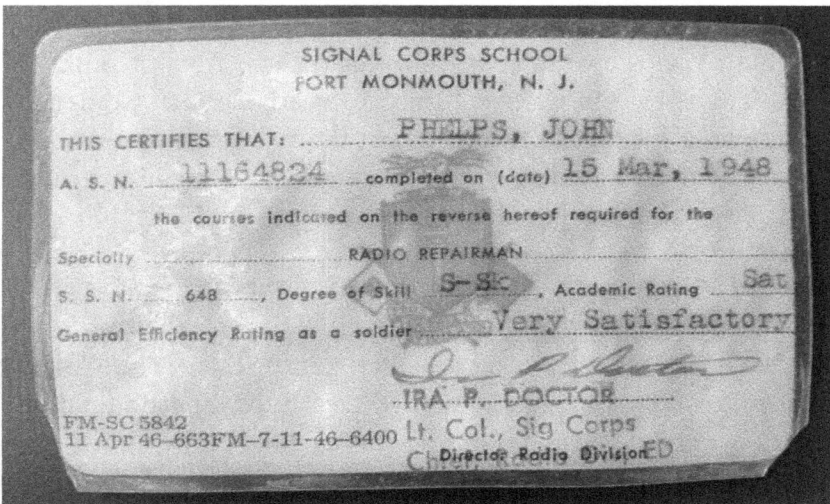

Never heard of the Signal Corps? Here's some background. While serving as a medical officer in Texas in 1856, Albert James Myer proposed that the Army use his visual communications system called aerial telegraphy. The system known as "wig-wag" was adopted in June 1860 and the Signal Corps was born. Myer became the first and only Signal Officer. In 1863, it became official and Congress authorized a regular Signal Corps for the duration of the Civil War.[6] Myer began to train others as part of the professional military signal service. For the next 79 years the Signal Corps would

---

6. https://en.wikipedia.org/wiki/Signal_Corps_(United_States_Army)

support the Armed Forces with communication support for every military engagement. When the War Department was reorganized in 1942, the Signal Corps became one of the technical departments in the Services of Supply. Its organized components served both the Army Ground Forces and the Army Air Forces. The Signal Corps has always been an innovator in communication. In 1946, its Project Diana successfully bounced radar signals off the moon, paving the way for space and satellite communications.

Back to Stan's late father. John graduated Signal Corps school and became a radio repairman stationed at Hickam Air Force Base in Hawaii. The base in Oahu was next to Pearl Harbor. As a repairman, one of his main jobs was to test the strength and readability of radio signals. Specifically, they were judging volume and clarity using a signal strength and readability report.

A signal strength and readability report is a standardized format for reporting the strength of a radio signal and the readability (quality) of the radiotelephone (voice) or radiotelegraph (Morse code) signal transmitted by another station as received at the reporting station's location and by their radio station equipment. Following is a chart representing the scale.

The scale was from 1-5. The number one represented the worst and five was the best. The first number in the scale represented the signal strength and the second number represented the signal clarity. If both strength (volume) and clarity were excellent, the receiver would reply "five by five." That was shorthand for "I understand you perfectly." We reference this scale today when we say "loud and clear."

Today, five by five has found its way into verbal slang, meaning "everything is good" or "everybody is well/good."[7]

---

7. https://www.urbandictionary.com/define.php?term=5%20x%205

Proword	Meaning		Proword	Meaning
LOUD	Your signal is very strong.	5	CLEAR	The quality of your transmission is excellent.
GOOD	Your signal strength is good.	4	READABLE	The quality of your transmission is satisfactory.
WEAK	Your signal strength is weak.	3	UNREAD-ABLE	The quality of your transmission is so bad that I can barely read you.
VERY WEAK	Your signal strength is very weak.	2	DISTORT-ED	Having trouble reading you due to distortion.
FADING	At times your signal strength fades to such an extent that continuous reception cannot be relied upon.	1	WITH INTER-FERENCE	Having trouble reading you due to interference.

We believe that the five by five framework is ideally suited for presenting. Our goal when presenting is to come across "Loud" and "Clear." In Section II of this book, we'll examine the five keys of rising above distractions when presenting and the five keys of creating clear content that's memorable.

CONDUCTIVITY

Another reason for choosing silver to represent presentation communication is its conductivity. Silver exhibits the highest electrical conductivity and thermal conductivity of any metal.

Electrical conductivity is a measure of movable atoms known as free electrons. For a material to be a good conductor, the electricity passed through it must be able to move the electrons. The more free electrons in a metal, the greater its conductivity. Silver contains a greater number of movable atoms compared to other metals.[8]

Thermal conductivity is a measure of the ability of heat to pass through a material. Materials with a high thermal conductivity can effectively transfer heat and readily take up heat from their environment. Silver has the highest thermal conductivity of any metal.

Why do we think conductivity matters? As a presenter, you are the conduit between the information and the audience.

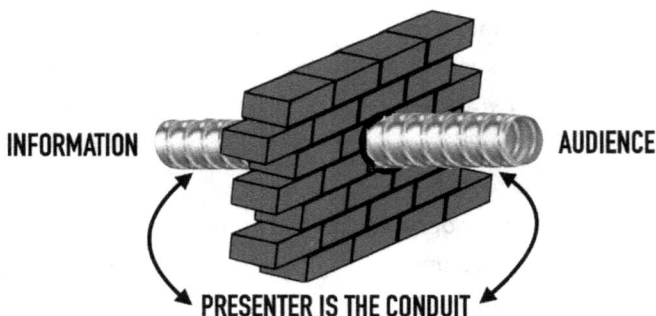

INFORMATION   AUDIENCE

PRESENTER IS THE CONDUIT

---

8. https://sciencing.com/metals-make-good-conductors-electricity-8115694.html

Your goal as a presenter is to allow that information to be transferred in the best possible way. You as the presenter are responsible for creating the connection. You're the conduit on stage.

POLISHABILITY

Silver has the ability to show a brilliant metallic luster. The etymology of silver has a Proto-Indo-European root (*$h_2erǵ$- formerly reconstructed as *$arǵ$-), meaning "shining."[9] Given its luster, silver can take a high polish. It can give off a brilliant shine. Unfortunately, it also tarnishes very easily. In the words of Lyndsie Selwyn:

> When silver is exposed to sulfur-containing gases in the air, it discolors and then darkens as it reacts with the gas to form a surface layer of tarnish. This process is called tarnishing. . . . Tarnish generally disfigures a silver object. It can be removed by polishing or other techniques, but this cleaning can be labor intensive. Moreover, each time an object tarnishes and is cleaned, some silver is lost.[10]

Polishability also has a direct application to presentation skills. No one is born a great presenter. You need to constantly work on improving and polishing your delivery/organizational skills. Those sulfur-containing gases in the air represent all of the bad presentations in this world. The more of those you see and mimic, the more your skills begin to tarnish. You don't want to dull your shine so learn how to avoid them. Stephen Covey would refer to this polishing as "sharpening the saw."

Next, we'll examine the metaphor of a goldfish and the simple idea that "little things" can make the biggest difference.

---

9. https://tied.verbix.com/project/phonetics/word29.html
10. https://www.canada.ca/en/conservation-institute/services/workshops-conferences/regional-workshops-conservation/understanding-silver-tarnish.html

CHAPTER 3

WHY A GOLDFISH?

"Big doors swing on small hinges."

— W. Clement Stone

Why a goldfish in the *Silver Goldfish* title? The origin of the goldfish as a symbol dates back to 2012 when it became the signature of this book series. The goldfish is a metaphor that represents something small that, despite its size, can make a big difference.

For example, Kimpton Hotels are famous for the attention they put on guest experience. The hotel chain has a number of signature additions that go above and beyond expectations. If you stay at a Kimpton, you can count on there being free gourmet coffee and fresh fruit in the lobby 24 hours a day. In the afternoon they host a wine tasting. Not samples—full glasses of specially selected wine. Some Kimpton hotels will let you take out a bike for free to tour the city. All Kimptons are pet-friendly. Bring your dog for free and they'll treat your pup like royalty.

Our favorite little extra was introduced by Kimpton at each Hotel Monaco back in 2001. Perhaps you are staying at a Kimpton and getting a little lonely. Or maybe you and your family are away from home and missing your pet. The program is called Guppy Love. It offers guests the opportunity to adopt a temporary travel companion—a goldfish—for the duration of their stay. This unique program gained the chain national attention. Steve Pinetti, Senior Vice President of Sales & Marketing for Kimpton Hotels and Restaurants, shared:

> The 'Guppy Love' program is a fun extension of our pet-friendly nature as well as our emphasis on indulging the senses to heighten the travel experience. Everything about Hotel Monaco appeals directly to the senses, and 'Guppy Love' offers one more unique way to relax, indulge and promote the health of mind, body, and spirit in our home-away-from-home atmosphere.

The second reason for the symbolism of a goldfish has to do with Stan's childhood. At age six, his first pet was a goldfish named Oscar.

He won it at a fair by throwing a ping pong ball in a carnival game. Oscar was small, maybe an inch in length. It turns out that the average goldfish is just over three inches. Yet the longest in the world is just under 20 inches. Not a carp or a koi, but an ordinary goldfish. That's more than six times the average size. The same thing applies to presenters. Some presenters are average

FACT

The current *Guinness Book of World Records* holder for the largest goldfish hails from the Netherlands at a whopping 19 inches (50 centimeters). To put that in perspective, that's about the size of the average domesticated cat.

Six times larger!!! Imagine walking down the street and bumping into someone who's nearly three stories tall. How can there be such a disparity between your garden variety goldfish and their monster cousins?

It turns out that the growth of the goldfish is determined by five factors. And those same five factors also relate to the growth of any business and/or salesperson.

Let's unpack the five factors:

#1. The first growth factor for a goldfish is the **SIZE OF THE ENVIRONMENT** they are in. The size of the bowl or pond is one determinant of how much they will grow. The size is a direct correlation. The larger the bowl or pond, the larger the goldfish can grow. The smaller the market, the lesser the growth. In business, what's the equivalent of the bowl or the pond? It's simply the **MARKET** for your product or service.

Takeaway: The bigger the market, the more you can grow.

#2. The second growth factor for a goldfish is the **NUMBER OF OTHER GOLDFISH** in the environment. This is an inverse correlation. The more goldfish in the bowl or pond, typically the less growth achieved. With fewer goldfish, the more growth opportunities. Who are the other goldfish in business? They are your **COMPETITION**.

Takeaway: The more competition, the harder it is to grow. The less competition, the easier it is to grow.

#3. The third growth factor is the **QUALITY OF THE WATER** that the goldfish is in. Nutrients and cloudiness in the water will impact the growth of a goldfish. The better the quality—the more nutrients and less cloudiness in the water—the more growth. Conversely, fewer nutrients and more cloudiness will hamper growth. What is the equivalent of the quality of water in business? Here we need to think in a macro and environmental sense. The quality of the water is the **ECONOMY**. It is a direct correlation.

Takeaway: The better the quality of the economy and the greater consumer confidence, the larger the growth. The weaker the economy or capital markets, the more difficult it is to access capital and grow.

#4. The fourth factor for a goldfish is how they're treated in the **FIRST 120 DAYS** of life. The nourishment and treatment they receive as babies are key to future growth. Goldfish are tiny when they are born, usually with about a hundred brothers and sisters. They are about the size of the head of a pin. What do you call a baby goldfish? A baby goldfish is a fry, as in "small fry." The lower the quality of the food and treatment, the more the goldfish will be stunted for future growth. What's the equivalent of the first 120 days in business? A business is typically called a **START-UP** during its early days in business.

FACT

A malnourished goldfish in a crowded, cloudy environment may only grow to two inches (five centimeters).

Takeaway: How a start-up does in the first four months of its existence will be a determining factor of how it will do in the long term.

#5. The fifth and final growth factor for a goldfish is **GENETIC MAKEUP**. The strength of its genetics will determine future growth. The stronger its genes and the more it is separated from the rest of the goldfish, the more it typically grows. The poorer the genes and the more it hangs out in the same goldfish group, the less it can grow. What's the equivalent of genetic makeup in business? It is **DIFFERENTIATION**.

Takeaway: The more differentiated the product or service from the competition, the better the chance for growth. The less differentiated and the more a business is like the competition, the harder it will be to grow.

WHICH OF THE FIVE FACTORS CAN YOU CONTROL?

Let's assume you have an existing product or service and have been in business for more than four months. Which of the remaining four factors do you have control over?

1. Size of the bowl = Market

2. Number of other goldfish = Competition

3. Quality of water = Economy

4. Genetic makeup = Differentiation

Do you have any control over the market, your competition, or the economy? NO, NO, and NO. The only thing you have control over is your genetic make-up or how you differentiate what you do and how you do it. In sales, how do you stand out in a sea of sameness?

In summary, the goldfish in *Silver Goldfish* represents differentiation. How do you stand out by doing the little things that improve your ability as a presenter? And the silver in *Silver Goldfish* symbolizes how well you rise above the noise and clarify your message. How you become the conduit for your message to come across "Loud" and "Clear." How you polish your skills and not fall victim to tarnish.

Next, we'll look at the idea of finding a silver bullet in communication.

CHAPTER 4

SILVER BULLET

"There is no silver bullet and frankly you probably don't need one. It is far more important to be able to find the right kind of gun, be able to load the gun . . . and perhaps most importantly, be able to figure out where the werewolf is."

— Matthew Oliphant

I n folklore, silver was commonly thought to have mystic pow-
ers. For example, a bullet cast from silver is often supposed to
be the only weapon that is effective against a werewolf, witch,
or other monsters. In the 1950s *Lone Ranger* series, the namesake
used a silver bullet as his calling card for law and justice.

A silver bullet has come to symbolize "a simple, seemingly magical, solution to a difficult problem."[11] Over the years, the idiom of a
silver bullet has developed to refer to any simple solution with very
high effectiveness or almost miraculous results. Based on the most
basic observations of the business world, presenting well should
certainly qualify as a difficult problem. What then is the silver
bullet?

It turns out silver makes bad bullets. Its density is less than that of
lead, making a silver bullet less accurate, less deadly, and more ex-
pensive than a "normal" bullet. Even the television show *Mythbusters*
agrees, so you know it's true.[12]

There is no magical solution for the difficult problem of presenting well. It takes thought, work, and the ability to be different to
stand out in that sea of sameness. No one was born with the ability to wow an audience. It's a learned behavior. It's a skill. Those
who work at it become better than those who don't. It's not ter-
ribly complicated, but it is incredibly difficult. Those who master
the skill will reap the rewards of audience attention, engagement,
and response. Frequently that mastery results in job opportunities,
contracts, and Twitter followers.

But that doesn't stop people from looking for the magic elixir. The
number one phone call received at MillsWyck Communications is
someone asking if we can make them a confident speaker. Most are
shocked when the answer is no.

---

11. https://en.wikipedia.org/wiki/Silver_bullet
12. https://mythresults.com/episode79

Confidence is the belief in an ability. NBA players who shoot free throws successfully 90+ percent of the time want the ball. Hand it to the guy shooting 37 percent and he acts like the ball has the Coronavirus. If you're bad at something, why would you be confident? When teenagers learn to drive, they are (or at least should be) scared. They're a danger to themselves and everyone else on the road. But after a few years of accident-free driving, they'll venture out at rush hour on a multi-lane highway and come back safe. Their confidence soars. Confidence follows competence. This is also true of speaking as well. Virtually no one who has a confidence problem in speaking has become good at it.

Presenters left untrained don't usually get better. They muddle on, driven by some sadistic force or the inability to say "no." Many confess they get physically ill before a big meeting. One confessed she had changed jobs three times to avoid having to make presentations. They all want a quick fix. They'll be disappointed.

Here's the first bad news we have to share:

THERE IS NO SILVER BULLET TO PRESENTING WELL

Speaking is a skill. Presenting better is attainable for anyone who is willing to work at it. Just like driving, just like time management, just like golf, and just like being a good parent. But working at it and doing it more are not the same thing. Spending 10 years flipping burgers does not make you a master chef. It means you spent a decade doing something we can train a teenager to do in 15 minutes.

If getting better is possible, what do we need to do? It's simple. And it's hard. But let's start with the simple. You're well on your way. You've made it to chapter 4. That alone is an indication that you can be successful.

Here's the second piece of bad news:

YOU WEREN'T BORN WITH A SILVER TONGUE

According to the website Grammarist,

> Silver-tongued is a description of someone who expresses himself in a clever manner, someone who is well-spoken, someone who speaks eloquently. Synonyms of the idiom silver-tongued that may be found in a thesaurus are articulate, glib, well-spoken. The term silver-tongued has been in use since at least the 1590s, and comes from an obscure definition of the word silver. Silver may be used to describe something melodious and resonant, a reference to the pleasing sound of ringing silver. Many attribute the term silver-tongued to a description of a certain preacher who lived in England in the latter 1500s named Henry Smithe, also known as Silver Tongued Smith. However, there is a passage in the Old Testament of the Bible which may be the basis of this idiom. The pertinent passage in Proverbs 10:20 is "The tongue of the righteous is as choice silver; the heart of the wicked is worth little."[13]

You weren't born with a silver tongue, but you can work toward becoming articulate and well-spoken when presenting.

TWO SIMPLE TRUTHS

The first simple truth is that your audience needs to hear you. There are lots of distractions competing for their attention. Their phone may be the biggest. You need to be "Loud." We're not talking about your voice's volume, although that also may be an issue, but

---

13. https://grammarist.com/idiom/silver-tongued/

about the compelling nature of making people want to tune in to what you are saying.

Next, what you say needs to be crystal clear. This isn't about your diction or your microphone. This is about a transfer of a message. No confusion. No misinterpretation. No misquoting later on. Three simple words:

Loud. And. Clear.

Again, there is no silver bullet. In the words of Matthew Oliphant, "There is no silver bullet and frankly you probably don't need one. It is far more important to be able to find the right kind of gun, be able to load the gun . . . and perhaps most importantly, be able to figure out where the werewolf is." The werewolf represents your upcoming presentation. We're going to show you how to create and deliver great presentations for any audience and situation.

Let's look at the 10 keys to make you stand out when presenting.

LOUD AND CLEAR
(THE WHAT)

CHAPTER 5

OVERVIEW

"Communication is a skill that you can learn. It's like riding a bicycle or typing. If you're willing to work at it, you can rapidly improve the quality of every part of your life."

— Brian Tracy

In this section we'll explore the 10 keys to effective communication. These 10 keys will help to develop your presentation skills and generally will serve you well. In the words of Warren Buffet, "One of the things you want to be sure to do, whether you like it or not, is get comfortable with public speaking. That's an asset that will last you 50 or 60 years. It's a necessary skill." Our focus on these 10 keys will be on the skills needed to develop content and present with distinction in a corporate setting. How to come across Loud and Clear.

WHY 10 KEYS?

As we shared in the "Why Silver" chapter, the inspiration for five by five comes from the military. When communicating via radio, it was always important to judge the strength of the signal. There are two measures: Volume + Clarity. Each was judged on a scale of 1 to 5, with 5 being the best. If the signal was excellent, the response was five by five. This indicated you were loud and clear. With that in mind, we are sharing five keys for volume and five keys for clarity for improving your presentation communication.

Here's how each of the five break down over the next 10 chapters:

Loud (being heard above distractions)

1. Impress

2. Connect

3. Express

4. Facilitate

5. Entertain

Clear (clarity of your message)

1. Simplification

2. Organization

3. Objective

4. Visualize

5. Time

Let's begin on how to make a great first impression.

CHAPTER 6

IMPRESS

"We don't know where our first impressions come from or precisely what they mean, so we don't always appreciate their fragility."

— Malcolm Gladwell

Walk into any room and there will be ambient noise: the hum of an air conditioner, the tick of a wall clock, the shuffling of feet, and the screeching of chairs across the floor. A speaker has to be louder than all of that. More importantly, the speaker must be LOUD—as in more interesting than all the other noises that exist inside the heads of the audience. The audience will tune you out for the simplest of reasons.

Will Rogers is quoted to have said, *"You never get a second chance to make a first impression."* The same quote is also attributed to Oscar Wilde. But the earliest use in print can be attributed to Madison Avenue in a 1966 advertisement for Botany Suits.[14] Regardless of the origin, the importance of getting off on the right foot is paramount. The first impression you create is extremely important when it comes to presenting.

Here are six things you should be address of when making that first impression.

INTRODUCTION

Introductions are crucial to effective presentations because an audience assesses the caliber of a presenter right from the start. According to Kim Harrison, "A rule of thumb suggests that an audience's assessment of a speaker is largely formed in the first 30 seconds." You can get off to a good start by making sure you have a proper introduction.[15]

TIP #1 (TIP as in "To Improve Presentations") - Don't leave your intro to chance. Provide a short, well-written bio to the person introducing you as a presenter.

---

14. http://answers.google.com/answers/threadview?id=438532
15. https://cuttingedgepr.com/free-articles/important-introduce-speaker-well/

DRESS

Whether we like it or not, our appearance matters when presenting. Perhaps it shouldn't, but it does. We judge people in a split-second. Over 80 percent of those judgments come down to just two factors. Fellow speaker and author of *The Human Brand* Chris Malone explains the phenomenon:

> Early humans developed a kind of genius for making two specific kinds of quick judgments: What are the intentions of other people toward me? And how capable are they of carrying out those intentions? Social psychologists call these two categories of perception WARMTH and COMPETENCE, and they drive most of our emotions and behavior toward other people.[16]

Before a word comes out of your mouth when presenting, people have made judgments about you. How you dress drives those perceptions. You never get a second chance to impact those crucial first impressions. Once that impression is made, confirmation bias begins. Our brain begins the process of looking for clues to confirm that initial impression.

"To paraphrase Coco Chanel: Dress shabbily and they remember the dress/clothes. Dress impeccably and they remember the woman or man."

— Jennifer Pacilan

---

16. https://fidelum.com/book/

So, what's the solution?

Simple. You "dress to the nines." The origin of this commonly used phrase is unclear. We prefer the Old English version. The saying "dressed to the eyes," was often written as "dressed to then eyne." According to *Mental Floss*, "The thinking goes that someone at some point heard 'then eyne' and mistook it for 'the nine' or 'the nines.'"[17]

How are you dressing to the eyes to reinforce warmth and competence?

> Dress a touch above your average audience member. When Alan worked as a corporate trainer, he was in a very casual culture. Shorts and flip flops were the accepted norm. But as a speaker/trainer, when he learned this truth he wore slacks and a polo to teach. That hardly classified as formalwear, but it sent a message: I take this seriously and this is important. It was an incremental step toward becoming better.
>
> At a national convention, the director of a local nonprofit was given fifteen minutes to highlight her cause. She was passionate, articulate, and poorly dressed. Not stylistically. She was a fashion leader. But she had a shawl that would not stay put. She wasn't being indecent—she wore a fine blouse under the wrap. But when the shawl slipped off her shoulder, she would shift her whole body and grab it with her hand to hoist it back up. That wouldn't have been the death knell, but she did it with the hand
>
> *Continued . . .*

17. https://www.mentalfloss.com/article/49785/
    where-did-phrase-%E2%80%9Cdressed-nines%E2%80%9D-come

holding the mic. Which might not have been so bad had she not been wearing some 6-inch dangling earrings that got hit by the shawl about two inches from the mic each time she did this (and it happened at least twenty times in 15 minutes). Her cause was forgotten in the cacophony of loud clanging noise. She was not "Loud"— her earrings were.

Another factor to consider is being comfortable. If you're standing, then you need to be able to hold your ground without shifting and to walk easily without wincing or altering your gait. You may love those new stiletto heels, but if you can't walk up three steps to the stage in them, they probably aren't for presenting in.

In a live setting, our eyes adjust and can easily differentiate between the outfit and the background. But on video, where you are compressed into two dimensions, patterns and color take on even greater importance. In particular, you should avoid swirling patterns (like paisley), tight patterns (like checks), or narrow stripes. Tight patterns create an optical illusion called moiré that looks like it's moving. Avoid wild colors. Reds often bleed (are blurry) on video. Black and white is bland. Safe bets are solid pastels or primary colors. It would be great to know what the backdrop is going to be before you go on stage—a visit before your presentation or at least an inquiry to the event host is a good idea before you choose your outfit.

TIP #2 - The standard should be to dress appropriately and stylishly for the audience to make a positive first impression. Stan once heard a presenter share that their policy was to "dress to a tie." The point they were making was not to over or underdress for your audience. Dress similar to the audience or maybe a little bit better.

Speaker and consultant Rob Biesenbach says we should keep four things in mind:[18]

1. Dress to feel good

2. Dress to look good

3. Dress to the audience/venue

4. Dress to your brand

"We are often unaware of how certain aspects of our appearance come across to others. I would recommend to proactively seek out this kind of feedback. It's typically not provided voluntarily, so we unwittingly continue our usual habits, blissfully unaware of the message we are sending to others. As we used to say at Coca-Cola, 'Everything communicates!' "

— Chris Malone

FIRST WORDS

First impressions get reinforced once you start speaking. According to *Forbes*, they happen within the first seven seconds.[19] The audience will remember the first thing they hear. You need to hook

---

18. https://robbiesenbach.com/what-to-wear-for-a-presentation/
19. https://www.forbes.com/sites/serenitygibbons/2018/06/19/you-have-7-seconds-to-make-a-first-impression-heres-how-to-succeed/#5fb9e88a56c2

them right from the beginning. Start strong with a good story. Bill Stainton says, "Start with your second best story . . . finish with your best one."

Why? There is a concept in psychology called the serial position effect. It is more commonly referred to as the primacy and recency effect. Coined by the late Hermann Ebbinghaus, the concept implies that when people are asked to recall a list of items, they tend to be able to best recall those at the end of the list (the recency effect) and those at the beginning of the list (the primacy effect) better than those in the middle of the list.[20]

Later on, we'll teach you how you can relate the beginning and end to maximize the effects.

TIP #3 - Make the most of your first words. Same words used in second point. Here's a list of four things you want to avoid doing:

1. Don't open with your name.

2. Don't say "I'm happy to be here." Start strong with a good story that hooks your audience and gets them engaged.

3. Don't say "Before we get started . . ." You've already started.

4. Don't say "Thanks . . ." There are precious few instances where there needs to be a public thank you. Especially in your opening first few words. Occasionally maybe. But usually save them. Saying "thanks" doesn't move the needle on engagement.

---

20. https://www.socialmediatoday.com/content/
customer-relationships-and-primacy-and-recency-effect

"If you are trying to get information across to someone, your ability to create a compelling introduction may be the most important single factor in the success of your mission."

— Dr. John Medina

AVOID THE LIGHT

When presenting and using a projector with slides, avoid the tractor beam. Unlike Carol Anne in the classic 1980s movie *Poltergeist*, avoid the light. (Millennial and GenZ Update: little Carol Ann climbed into the television at the behest of a ghost in this classic horror movie.)

Here are three things you can do to avoid becoming a shadow puppet:

1. Masking tape - This is a great tip if you have an overhead projector. During set-up, move around to see where you begin to encroach on the light. Then mark the floor or table to avoid moving into that area.

2. Table it - If the projector is on a cart or table, then simply walk around it. The great news is that projectors have gotten better over the years. Short throw projectors have reduced the length of the beam.

3. Black out - Some clickers have a blackout button. Use it when you need to walk in front of the projector. One bonus tip when talking about clickers. Don't use the laser pointer. You are not a Jedi. Resist the urge, you must. Want to highlight something on your slide? Then do the proper work when

creating your slides. A tiny red or green dot isn't a substitute for your lack of planning, padawan.

TIP #4 - It's simple, be aware of the beam and don't walk in front of the projector.

BEST FACE FORWARD

Do not talk to the screen when presenting. You want to maintain eye contact and keep the audience engaged. Do not (ever) read your slides. People can read about four times faster than you can speak.[21] And unless you're a preschool teacher, your audience is literate. Don't insult the intelligence of your audience by reading to them.

TIP #5 - Face forward. Here are three hacks to keep your best face forward and on track when presenting:

1. Place your laptop in front of you and use Presenter Mode. This allows you to see the current slide on the projector or screen and the next slide or animation at the same time.

2. Ask for a confidence monitor. This is a small screen in front of you that shows what's on the screen behind you. It eliminates the need to look at the screen behind you.

3. Set up a tablet or phone in front of you in video mode. Face it toward the screen and, like a mirror, you can now see the screen behind you.

POSTURE

No one ever remarks about posture on an evaluation. "Man, that Stan. He had the straightest shoulders and most amazing balance I've ever seen." But the audience infers how you are feeling from your

---

21. https://courses.lumenlearning.com/ivytech-comm101-master/chapter/chapter-4-three-as-of-active-listening/

posture. Are you coming across as lazy, arrogant, defensive, nervous, or disengaged? It's easy to find postures that give wrong messages. The right message? Not so easy. So eliminate the bad and you're on your way to good. Remove anything that distracts or sends the wrong message. Here are some common bad postures to avoid:

| PARADE REST | HANDS IN POCKET | FOOTBALL COACH | WRIST RUBBER | ARMS CROSSED | SPIDER PUSH-UPS | FIG LEAF |

TIP #6 - You can't win with posture, but it can cause you to lose. Use neutral posture (arms relaxed, down at your sides) to remove distractions and send the most positive impression possible. Act like you want to be there. Your clients, your boss, your prospects, and your clients constantly form opinions based on your posture.

Authors' Note: Hands in pockets is OK in moderation.

NEUTRAL POSTURE
(ARMS RELAXED, DOWN AT YOUR SIDES)

"We judge ourselves based on our intent. Everyone else judges us based on our actions."

— Stephen Covey Jr.

What about when we are seated, like at a conference room table? Etiquette suggests our hands be visible on top of the table. In some cultures, hidden hands create distrust. Your hands need to be still. Clasp them. Stack them. Separate them. But don't twitch, drum your pencil, pick your nails, or move your hands except to gesture. Sit balanced, back off the chair, leaning forward. Act like you want to be there!

Next, let's look at the things you can do to create a better sense of connection when presenting.

CHAPTER 7

CONNECT

"It's not about perfection when presenting: it's about connection."

— Stephanie Scotti

G reat speakers connect with their audiences. They understand a simple truth: The audience wants you to succeed. They want to pay attention. They want you to capture their mind and heart—to be louder than the noise in their own head. They don't require you to be perfect. In the words of speaking coach Stephanie Scotti, "It's not about perfection when presenting; it's about connection." If you want to be a great presenter, you need to connect. Connection before content. And this might seem counterintuitive, but the first thing you need to do is STOP.

S.T.O.P.

This acronym is one of best speaking techniques for establishing connection. Coined by Andrew Gilman, here's how the acronym of S.T.O.P. works.[22] You deliver a **S**ingle **T**hought to **O**ne **P**erson. You think of and compose your next thought while finding a new person in the audience. You are not allowed to start delivering the thought until you establish eye contact. Then you deliver that next single thought. Lather, rinse, repeat.

Why S.T.O.P?

S.T.O.P. has four amazing benefits:

1. S.T.O.P. eliminates filler words. This may be the biggest benefit for the listener. Filler words (such as uh, um, and , so) automatically disappear. According to Susan Ward, "Using excessive fillers is the most irritating speech habit. They distract your listener often to the point that he or she doesn't hear anything you say."[23]

2. It allows you time to breathe by slowing you down. Breathing calms your nerves. It allows needed oxygen to your brain, making you smarter on your feet.

---

22. https://www.tesh.com/articles/how-do-you-break-the-habit-of-using-speech-tics/
23. https://www.toastmasters.org/magazine/articles/cutting-out-filler-words

3. It reinforces eye contact which allows your audience the ability to connect with you. The eyes are the window to the soul (Chinese proverb). You're seen as more trusted, you appear more confident, and you won't read your slides. S.T.O.P. also allows you to monitor your audience's response to what you are saying. They will feel like you are talking to them.

4. The pauses allow you to create flow and tempo. They also allow the audience to filter what you've just said. Our brains can't effectively multitask. The gaps between thoughts give the listener needed time to process the information.

TIP #7 - Start S.T.O.P.ing by both speaking and listening. Practice it in conversations. Use it when you rehearse your presentation. Then, listen for it. Especially when you have the radio on. The next time you hear an interview on the radio, listen for filler words. Notice the marked difference between the on-air personality and the person being interviewed.

In our speaker workshops, we begin by having participants introduce themselves. May as well ask them to speak on a topic they're an expert on! We ask them to speak for 90 seconds, and we don't let them finish early. There are two main reasons for this length. First, the instructor/coach is marking an evaluation sheet covering 14 specific skills, including counting all the non-words in the talk. We like to evaluate each skill twice, and that takes time. Second, we've found that anyone can memorize about 45 seconds of material. Most people have a 30-second networking pitch ready to go. Almost no one

Continued . . .

can go 90 seconds by memory. It forces them to come up with material on the fly. That's where we see the true skill set that is normal.

The average number of non-words in those 90 seconds? 18. There appears to be no difference between native English speakers and those using their second (or third or fourth) language. Only two students in about 5000 have gotten through 90 seconds with zero non-words.

WORK THE EDGES

Eye contact establishes connection. Most presenters make the mistake of only connecting with people in the middle of the room or only looking at people they know or like. Engage the entire audience.

TIP #8 - Address the edges of the room throughout your presentation.

STORY TIME

Want to connect when presenting? Then use stories. Why? Because "facts tell, stories sell." This quote by Bryan Eisenberg reinforces the importance of using the power of story when presenting. Stories make your message memorable. And memorability is the holy grail of presenting.

Here are three questions to ask about telling stories:

1. When should you use stories? Answer: Early and often.

2. How long should your stories be? Answer: It depends on the time you have. Practice stories with different levels of detail given different times. This allows you to manage time on the fly. Allow for three minutes, but have a one minute and a

five-minute version of the story as well. The moral/lesson of the story doesn't change. A rule of thumb when timing your opening story is no mor than 10 percent of the overall talk.

3. What's your role in the story? Answer: You are the guide. Donald Miller writes in the book *Building a StoryBrand,* "To enter into our customer's story, we should play the role of guide." The fatal mistake is positioning yourself as the hero in a story instead of the guide. You are Yoda, not Luke Skywalker.

Whether you are a fan of Disney, good literature, or the theater, you will see similarities to the storylines these genres use. Don't reinvent the wheel. Use the storytellers' system of keeping an audience engaged and the story moving toward its conclusion. The late Joseph Campbell modeled and described "The Hero's Journey." Inspired by mythology, the hero's journey occurs when something happens that causes the main character (hero) to go on a journey from the known to the unknown world. During this journey the hero learns a lesson and becomes transformed. The hero reemerges into the known world with greater knowledge from the journey. Nearly every Hollywood movie script follows this pattern.

Photo Credit: Wikipedia[24]

---

24. https://en.wikipedia.org/wiki/Hero%27s_journey#/media/File:Heroesjourney.svg

TIP #9 - Want to bring your stories to life? Then give them C.P.R. Not cardiopulmonary resuscitation, but a three-step formula:

1. **Challenge** - set the situation. What happened that created the challenge?

2. **Plan** - explain the actions taken. How did you address the challenge?

3. **Results** - summarize what you learned. What resulted from your actions?

> "In a recent presentation, I started a story—and then ended the presentation by finishing the story I had started at the beginning. I did it to build interest and suspense. Stories are important, because you can watch the audience perk up when you go from discussing a concept (an abstraction) to illuminating it with a real-world story (a concrete example of the abstraction)."
>
> — Laura Bergells

WIIFY

Even though you are at the front of the room as the presenter, it's not about YOU. It's about what's in it for the audience.

The solution is called W.I.I.F.Y., an acronym that stands for "What's In It For You" referencing the audience member. Why should they give you their attention? What value are you providing? What problem are you solving? Attention isn't given; it has to be earned.

W.I.I.F.Y. is more relevant now than ever. We live in a time when we are competing against constant distractions. We all know one thing that's a source of entertainment and constant stimulation. Something that the average person whips out an average of 58 times a day. We're talking about the smartphone. Our phones are always within arm's reach. And that's not going to change. In fact, according to research by the RescueTime app, few of us go longer than an hour during the day without touching our phones.[25]

Here are five ways to keep the smartphones at bay during a presentation:

1. Use stories - get your audience engaged early

2. Understand your audience - speak their language

3. Address their issues - know their pain

4. Deliver hope - be a light in the darkness

5. Offer a plan of action - provide a solution

Make sure you are commanding the attention of the audience when you present.

TIP #10 - When presenting, you need to be relevant and compelling to keep your audience tuned in.

Next, let's look at how to express when presenting.

---

25. https://blog.rescuetime.com/screen-time-stats-2018/

CHAPTER 8

EXPRESS

"The greatest form of expression—or, at least, the most common that we have as human beings, what separates us from the animals—is speaking: the ability to communicate."

— Chael Sonnen

J ust over 30 years ago, Madonna shared a bit of presenting advice. She challenged listeners to *"Express Yourself."* Part of being heard above the din of distraction is the skill of expressing yourself. And that begins with presence.

PRESENCE

You can't spell the word presentation without "present." And you can't be a good presenter without being present. Not the gift kind of present. But the "being present in the moment" form of presence. Perhaps the best advice on presence comes from Patsy Rodenburg. Rodenburg is a renowned British voice coach, author, and director known for her emphasis on expression and the primacy of the human voice. She established a framework called the Second Circle. According to her presentation on TED.com, it's a "state of mind and body where confident, relaxed control allows us to establish intimacy and human connection where and when we want it."[26]

Rodenburg describes three kinds of presence when we speak: first circle, second circle, and third circle. First circle presenters focus their energy inward. They are in their own head. Absorbed in their own thoughts and words, they minimize eye contact. In contrast, third circle presenters are bombastic and over-the-top. They focus their energy outward in order to dominate. They are loud and forceful. They can come across as telling rather than presenting. In between the first and third circle is the second circle. Second circle presenters have the right balance between self-awareness and presence for others. This is the ideal place you want to be when presenting. It's the right mix of connecting with the audience and expressing yourself.[27]

26. https://www.ted.com/speakers/patsy_rodenburg
27. https://www.forbes.com/sites/nickmorgan/2012/06/14/
    people-im-grateful-for-6-patsy-rodenburg/#56d806e8602e

THIRD CIRCLE

3 3

2 SECOND CIRCLE 2

FIRST CIRCLE

TELLING CONNECTED SELF 1 HEAD PRESENT LOUD

INWARD

2 2

3 PRESENT 3

OUTWARD

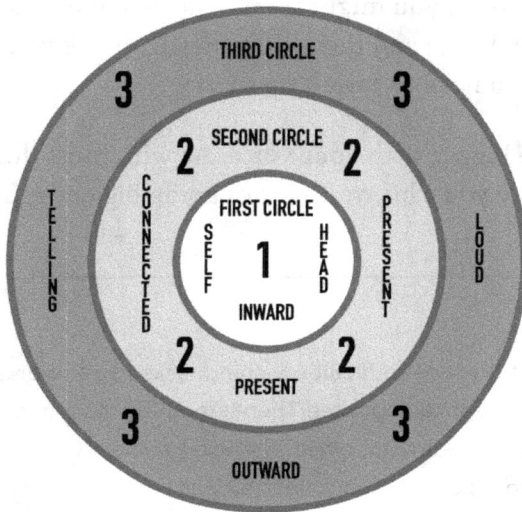

TIP #11 - Achieve the right balance when presenting. Spend the majority of your time in the second circle.

VOLUME

When presenting, it's important to vary the tone and volume of your voice. According to Nigel Tufnel, sometimes you need that "extra little push over the cliff." You need to take it up to 11. Not familiar with the concept of "One Louder" from *Spinal Tap*? Lead guitarist Nigel Tufnel (played by Christopher Guest) explains? to Director Marty DiBergi (played by Rob Reiner) how their amplifiers have a unique feature. He says, "Most amplifiers only go up to 10. These go to 11."[28]

Why is it important to turn it up with your volume when emphasizing key points?

It's because of a discounting effect. How you project (voice and gestures) when presenting is different from what your audience feels.

28. https://en.wikipedia.org/wiki/Up_to_eleven

On a scale of 1-10, you might think you are coming across as an 8. But ask the audience and they will generally judge you as a 5 or a 6. That's why you need to turn it up to 11.

TIP #12 - Go bigger with your voice. As with most things in life, if it doesn't scare you a bit, you are not going big enough.

> One of the most difficult coaching tasks in our workshops is a soft-spoken speaker. There's nothing wrong with being soft-spoken. But when it's time for them to get louder to empasize a certain point, the path is quite predictable. The coach wiill ask him to speak again, louder. The coach will ask what volume he thinks he's speaking at, and ask for still louder. And again. It's almost always the fourth or fifth time when the speaker will respond, "But I'm shouting." The other participants will laugh, politely. The presenter is a long way from shouting. It's a very instructive moment to have the entire group agree that there is still room for more volume while the speaker insists he is hurting people's eardrums. Simply put, we do not accurately hear ourselves.

PERSONAS

As you evaluate what we've been teaching about posture, volume, gestures, and presence, you might be tempted to say, "This feels like acting." It's a common response. But we usually love actors and actresses. We pay them lots of money to keep our attention. And that's what this behavior will do for you in a business presentation. Acting keeps your audience's attention. It makes you Loud—louder than the distractions they will otherwise want to entertain. Acting as a presenter is just being the person your audience needs you to be.

But acting needs purpose. It needs a character. When we visualize who we want to be like or who we want to reach, that is called a persona—a description of a fictional character.

Actors and actresses frequently spend months researching the characters they will play in a movie. Tom Hanks and the entire cast of *Saving Private Ryan* went through ten days of around-the-clock Marine boot camp prepping to film the movie.[29] The production crew of the animated film *Madagascar* spent a week camping in the African bush to understand the sights, sounds, and smells of the setting.

And you need to know who your audience needs you to be and study that character to become them. This isn't about faking them out or being someone you're not. It's about putting your best image forward so that your audience will trust and like you. If you are trying to be seen as a technical expert, perhaps you need to embrace standing your ground and not looking nervous. If you're inspiring youth, you probably need to bring some energy to your persona— you're competing with TikTok!

> My persona on stage (and when doing video) is "Super Viv." Sometimes you need to be a little "extra."
>
> — Viveka von Rosen

TIP #13 - Just like Beyoncé becomes Sasha Fierce and the late Kobe Bryant would become the Black Mamba, use a persona to amplify your presence and connect.

---

29. https://www.mentalfloss.com/
    article/65611/15-fascinating-facts-about-saving-private-ryan

GESTURES

One of the most common comments when presenters watch video of themselves is, "I never realized I move my hands so much." Ricky Bobby in *Talladega Nights* tells us why this is: "I'm not sure what to do with my hands." Are moving hands a good thing or a bad thing for presenters? The question is ill-formed and shows our misunderstanding. Moving your hands is not the goal. You want to *use* your hands to help convey your message. We call those movements gestures.

There are two aspects that make hand movement a gesture and not just moving your hands.

1. The movement adds meaning to your content. The easy way to judge this is to watch video with the sound turned off. If you can see meaning, then you have a gesture. If you just see hands moving—waving, twirling, up and down—then you just have movement. Gestures are a visual aid to what is being said.

2. The gesture needs to be away from the body. Gesturing is the extreme sport of presenting: Go big, or go home. Gestures begin at the shoulders, not the elbows. The basic rule here is that your elbows need to leave your sides. If possible, put your hands above your shoulders, away from your body.

How much gesturing should we do? There is no quota. But more than one a sentence is probably too much. Find a word that needs emphasis and dive right in to making it come alive with your whole body. Some words and phrases demand a gesture: Numbers below five. Any reference to something's size (big, small, tall). Directions and trends (northeast, up, lower). Actions that are easily displayed (typing, throwing, punching).

There are two main benefits of using big, appropriate gestures. The first is the most important. Your audience will have another channel of information supporting your content. If we ask your audience to remember what (correct) gestures you used, it will be easy for them to bring up the visual recall and repeat your message. If you stand still and motionless, they have only one channel—the auditory one. That's not easy for many audience members. The second is the natural change that big gestures make to your voice. That brings us to the next way to express yourself.

VOCAL VARIETY

It's not just about turning *up* the volume. Sometimes you need to tone it down. Creating that contrast makes the highs higher.

This largely depends on your natural voice. Some voices are louder than others. Naturally loud presenters can get attention when they soften their voice. A soft-spoken presenter cannot go softer. They won't be heard. They must find their level 11 volume. It's variety that keeps the attention of the audience.

"Most people just go with whatever they have, some want to do better so they turn up the volume and or speed. . . . the best know that that variance is the key."

— Dr. Todd Dewett

"Vary your speaking pace, volume, and pitch. Important points delivered slowly, softly and at a relaxed pitch (usually relatively low) often connect with audiences the most strongly and memorably."

— David Cervi

Consider professional voiceover specialists. They are paid for their professional voice. It has to be amazing. Fortunately, you don't have to imagine how they do this. YouTube will show you. Search for "Behind the scenes voiceover <insert your favorite animated movie>." You can watch Tim Allen, Ellen DeGeneres, Morgan Freeman, and Tom Hanks, and others show you the secret to changing your voice. Get the whole body involved. In short, act! Your voice (and audience) will thank you.

TIP #14 - Make sure you are varying the tone, volume, and tone of your voice. Think back to the three circles framework we shared earlier. In the first circle, you might be sharing something personal and dial it down to 3 or 4 on a scale of 1 to 10. Third circle moments require you to throttle it up. Opportunities when you provide a call to action or a powerful lesson might require you to turn it up to 10 or 11. Normal second circle of presence might be at 6 or 7.

EXPRESSING FEELINGS

When you are presenting, it's not only what you say but also how you say it. Especially when sharing feelings. What percentage do you think words convey when communicating something with feeling?

Only 7 percent.

It's called the Mehrabian effect. Coined by Albert Mehrabian, it's based on a study done back in 1967.[30] Mehrabian and his colleagues were seeking to understand the relative impact of facial expressions and spoken words.

Here's what he found when a subject was communicating something with feeling when there was a discrepancy between the

---

30. https://www.toolshero.com/communication-skills/communication-model-mehrabian/

words spoken and visual (nonverbal) clues apparent to the hearers:

- Words were believed 7 percent of the time.

- Vocal tone (volume, pace, tone) came in at 38 percent.

- Body language (gestures, facial expressions, movement) accounted for 55 percent of the believability.

Mehrabian published a book called *Silent Messages* where he explored all facets of nonverbal communication.

Author Note:

Mehrabian's work is sometimes associated with all communication. It's not. It's about the believability of a message when there are mixed signals. For instance, if I say I'm happy to be here, but do so with a gruff voice and arms crossed, what do you believe? What I said (I'm happy)? What you saw (arms crossed)? Or the tone of my voice (Grrrrr)? Consider pets and babies. Neither understands your words. But they respond to how you say things. Smile with a cooing voice and the baby thinks you love her no matter what you say ("You disgusting poop-producing fiend. Please, I'm begging you, sleep through the night tonight.") Google "Mehrabian Myth" to find out why this doesn't apply to ALL communication.

TIP #15 - When you present, understand those times when you tap into feelings. Realize that it's not just about what you say. More importantly it's also what your gestures and tone communicate.

> "Tone and body language are a huge part of communication. It's why the communication via texts, emails and online can get misread so easily."
>
> — Dave Crenshaw
>
> "One of the practices I've implemented for myself to improve [on] this, as well as [to help] my speaking coaching clients, is [to] watch video of our presentation without the sound on. It freaks you out to watch it, but tells its own story. Add in the words and it's incredible what the communication lessons are."
>
> — Jason Hewlett

BE REMEMBER-ABLE

The goal of presenting is to express yourself in order to communicate your message. You need to be remember-able. It's about communicating in a way that is easy to remember.

Sometimes it comes down to words we use. The absolute right words.

Mark Twain was asked by George Bainton for advice on writing. Twain's reply appeared in the book *The Art of Authorship* in 1890.

According to Quote Investigator, Twain presented a vividly comical contrast while discussing word selection. He said:[31]

> . . . the difference between the almost right word and the right word is really a large matter—'tis the difference between the lightning-bug and the lightning.

Twain credited the genesis of this quote to Josh Billings. Twain said, "He too was a great card on the lecture platform in those days; and his quaint and pithy maxims were on everybody's tongue."

In early 2019, Stan had the opportunity to visit Pearl Harbor. One item on display was a draft of Franklin Delano Roosevelt's (FDR) speech about the attack. FDR changed, "a date which will live in world history" to "a date which will live in infamy." That simple change made the speech more remember-able.

TIP #16 - Word up and become remember-able.

"Remember-able is better than 'merely memorable' is a powerful example of making more sticky word choices!"

— Laura Bergells

"Tapping into emotions has a powerful dual effect in concert with just hearing. So my goal is always to offer decent content and deliver it in a way that makes it stick emotionally."

— Todd Dewett, PhD

---

31. https://quoteinvestigator.com/2019/09/02/lightning/

USING DATA

Data is everywhere. Technical people love data. Facts. Figures. Percentages. Trends. For those who understand the data, it is proof positive that what they're saying is true. But for those who don't know the context or the subject matter, data can be confusing and may even say something entirely contrary to what the speaker wishes it did.

In the information age, mere data is useless. Anyone can find any fact they want in 30 seconds or less if they have an internet connection. In the old days, you needed a college education and access to a library or an expert to find information. But now information is readily available. Data is not compelling. What is compelling is the insight. The inside meaning of that data. That takes experience, a keen eye toward analysis, and an ability to apply your topic and data to your audience. We're certainly not against using data. But we like it to be used properly.

When using data, here are three questions that help an audience make sense of it:

1. Is it big or small?

   As you read the following statistics, try to determine if the numbers are big or small: 22.6 billion dollars, a 5.2 percent increase in budget, 0.48 percent of the total budget. In your mind, are these numbers big or small? The answer should be that it depends on what context you try to apply them to. We'll go out on a limb and guess that you think 22 billion dollars is a lot. A 5.2 percent increase over last year might depend—if you're looking at bonds you might think it's large. If you're a startup looking at growth, it's dreadfully small. Receiving 0.48 percent of a budget may sound small unless you know the budget is quite large.

   It turns out that these data points are all the same. They're a different representation of NASA's annual budget. Yes,

22.6 billion dollars is a lot of money, but it's only 0.48 percent of the entire federal budget, and it's only a 5.2 percent increase over what it was last year. You can make the case that it's big and ask for that money to be reallocated into education, defense, public works, or whatever your pet project is. You also could make the case that it's a small number compared to the defense budget or to government assistance programs.

This demonstrates the data can be used to make any point you want it to make. You can give the audience the impression that the number is big or small by simply using your gestures. If you hold your fingers close together and squint your eyes, you can make any number seem small. Put your arms as far apart as they'll go and use a big voice and any number can seem large. Most people don't know the difference between 22 billion and 23 billion, so the number itself is inconsequential. It's whether it seems big or small that matters to the audience. Give them that clarification.

2. Is it expected or unexpected? What's the trend and history of the data?

Knowing the history of the number is also important. Going back to the NASA budget, it has stayed almost flat for the last 30 years. The only time NASA's budget grew very much at all was in the 1960s when Apollo was trying to get a man to the Moon in less than a decade. But since the early 1970s, the NASA budget has hovered at between half a percent and one percent of the federal budget. It's gotten a few ticks upward and has been knocked down a little depending on which administration priorities are in play. When the graph[32] is displayed, the current year's budget doesn't seem all that noteworthy.

32. https://en.wikipedia.org/wiki/Budget_of_NASA#/media/File:NASA-Budget-Federal.svg

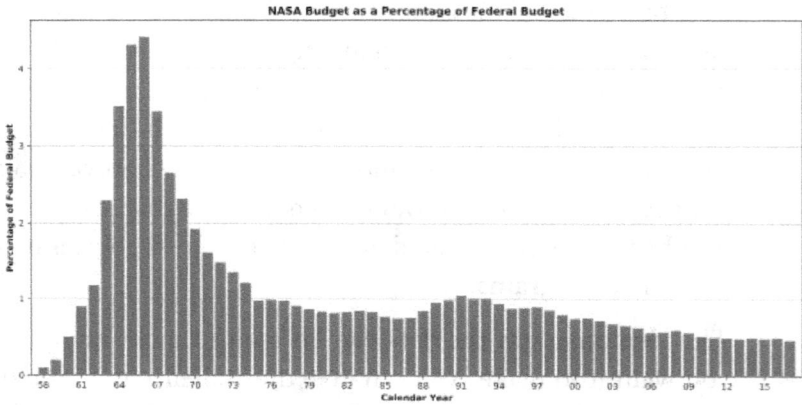

NASA Budget as a Percentage of Federal Budget

3. What does it mean to the audience?

Whether a number is big or small or whether it is trending up or down pales in comparison to what the number means to the audience. Here's where context, background, importance, and values matter to your audience. If you're giving a pro-space speech, then what matters about that 22 billion dollars is the return on investment, the technology we get, or the national pride that results from seeing our flag on the moon or on the side of a rocket that successfully launched. If you're anti-space, then the meaning of that money is that it diverts funds you believe are better used elsewhere. The annual NASA budget is more than the total endowment for all but two of the nation's universities (Harvard and Yale[33]). That much money could fund close to 400,000 public school teachers or feed every homeless person in the United States for 13 years. If you knew the hot topic for your audience, then such comparisons would give them context and meaning.

Here is where the presenter has a huge advantage over his or her audience. People will hear what you tell them to hear most of the time. Show them what the numbers mean and they walk away

33. https://nces.ed.gov/fastfacts/display.asp?id=73

repeating what the numbers mean to you. Politicians use this tactic all the time, citing statistics to support their cause and watching thousands of retweets flood the Internet.

TIP #17 - Don't just share data. Use size, expectation, and relevance to make it pop.

Next, let's examine how to best facilitate when presenting.

CHAPTER 9

FACILITATE

"The facilitator's job is to support everyone to do their best thinking and practice. To do this, the facilitator encourages full participation, promotes mutual understanding and cultivates shared responsibility."

— Sam Kaner

When you want to be Loud—heard above distractions—a key skill is handling the noise of your environment to keep the attention of your audience. You need to make it easy for them to pay attention. That's the definition of facilitate: to make easier; to help bring about.[34]

There's a long list of things that can go wrong and create distractions: technical difficulties (Wi-Fi connections, projector bulbs), audience problems (hecklers, people getting sick, audience leaving to watch ice melt), presenter problems (forgotten lines, slips of the tongue, wardrobe malfunctions, headache, revengeful dinner), wild or unwanted animals (mice, birds), facility issues (power outage, water leaking through the roof) and ambient noise (leaf blower outside, trumpet blaring next door, jackhammer in wall). We've experienced all of these while speaking on stage. There is no way you can prevent or expect every occurrence, no matter how thorough your preparation. But here are an even dozen of things you can do to manage the environment and minimize the distractions for your audience:

POSITIONING

Position yourself strategically. If possible, don't put yourself near doors and windows. People come in and out of doors and distractions are easily seen through windows. It's better to have a door at the rear of the room to allow people to come and go without attracting attention.

TIP #18 - Present from the front of the room and away from doors/windows.

BACKUP

Always—ALWAYS—have an analog backup to a digital solution. You should absolutely have backups to your files on a USB stick,

---

34. https://www.merriam-webster.com/dictionary/facilitate

cloud-based storage, and on your computer. But none of that will help you if your disk crashes, the web goes bust, the power goes out, or the projector bulb is kaput (and there is no spare). As you create your presentation, plan for what you'd do if you could not use your digital assets. Paper never goes out of style. The show must go on. If you couldn't present because your display adaptor had a faulty wire, that's a silly reason to lose a sale.

TIP #19 - Be prepared and always have a backup.

SOUND

Learn how to use a microphone. The mute button is your friend if you're not on stage. YouTube "Naked Gun Sound of Relief" if you wonder why. Don't forget to turn the mic back on when you take the stage! Most handheld mics are designed to be mounted on your chin and spoken across—not into. Park that sucker right on your chin and don't wave it at your audience. Sound going in and out or that is not able to be heard makes you look like a rookie, and you don't want to be remembered for what they *didn't* hear you say.

TIP #20 - Test your microphone before your presentation.

FIND HELP

Find a helper. Arrive early and ask a person to be your gopher if you need one. They'll say yes. Offer a Starbucks gift card to sweeten the deal. But it's just plain weird when you have to excuse yourself to get a drink, find the AV tech, or ask the sponsor when lunch is. Send the gopher instead.

TIP #21 - Ask for a helper.

GET TO IT

Don't talk about talking. That's our favorite way to describe silly phrases that serve little or no purpose. "I'm going to tell a story now

..." or "I heard this joke . . ." or "Let me tell you about . . . " or "I was just going to say . . . " Just say it.

TIP #22 - Don't talk about it. Jump in and get started.

USE NOTES

Make and take presenter notes and use them. They'll save you anxiety and save your bacon if you need them. But they should be used correctly. Their purpose is to remind you of what to say. You don't need a sentence to do that. Only a phrase. Find that phrase, then look up and speak to your audience. NEVER READ YOUR NOTES. Use them strategically. Take several copies and lay them on tables if you are going to move about the stage.

TIP #23 - Notes are fine. Use them, but don't abuse them.

NO "THANK YOU"

Stop the incessant litany of thank-you messages. Certain cultures like to be thanked. Cover the minimum. But thanking the person who invited you, the caterer, the interviewing manager, or the company admin who booked your flight should be done in person, with a note, or a gift. Not in front of your audience.

TIP #24 - Spare your audience. Keep the thank you messages to a minimum.

NO EXCUSES

Excuses sound empty from a leader or presenter. If you legitimately made a mistake that hurt or inconvenienced someone (like spilled coffee on them), then of course you apologize. But if you mispronounce a word or hit the spacebar twice instead of once, there is no apology needed.

TIP #25 - Don't make excuses.

NO INTRODUCTIONS NECESSARY

Stop the round robin audience introductions. Sales teams are especially enamored with everyone introducing themselves. But they take a long time and no one seems that interested. Establish your own credibility in your presentation, not the opening.

TIP #26 - Skip the intros.

KNOW THY AUDIENCE

Find out what they care about, already know, want to know, want to avoid, and understand the culture of the participants. Nowhere is this tougher than on a webinar or virtual meeting, but it's the presenter's job to know.

TIP #27 - Know your audience.

At a technical conference, an invited keynote speaker was scheduled for after the morning technical talk. Her opening line? "After listening to that, I realized I have no idea what you people do." Immediately almost every phone in the place came out as people completely ignored her presentation.

BEHAVE

Even the person who isn't on stage needs to behave. If you're part of a team or waiting your turn to present, people are watching. And remember, the audience always remembers the speaker, even if you don't remember the audience. Your behavior when you are not on stage matters. People draw opinions. If you chat through other talks or doze off or look disinterested, it reflects poorly on you and may very well change how people respond to you.

TIP #28 - Behave on and off stage.

MANAGE THE UNEXPECTED

Despite following every tip in this book (and any others), there will still be unexpected events that happen during your pitch, presentation, or interview. It's called Murphy's Law. "Anything that can go wrong, will go wrong."

So, who is this Murphy guy anyway and why is he always mucking things up? We need to fly over Edwards Air Force Base in 1949 to find out. According to the Murphys-Law.com rather than Murphy:[35]

> Capt. Edward Murphy [was] an engineer working on Air Force Project MX981, a project designed to see how much sudden deceleration a person can stand in a crash. One day, after finding that a transducer was wired wrong, he cursed the technician responsible and said, 'If there is any way to do it wrong, he'll find it.

TIP #29 - One thing you can do is to prepare. At some point in your presenting career Murphy will appear and your slides will disappear due to no fault of your own. To prep for that, Stan always has a one-page list in his pocket when presenting. Written with a sharpie, it looks like a setlist for a band. At any point, he can pull it out and have no problem staying on track. He also will always have a handheld microphone nearby.

What happens when we are faced with these setbacks? There are four typical responses.

---

35. http://www.murphys-laws.com/murphy/murphy-true.html

The first reaction may be the worst. We give up and don't try to cope. This is a flight response. The mindset is if we don't try or if we find others to blame, then it doesn't feel that bad.

The second response is anger. But it's hard to perform effectively when we are angry.

The third response is to try too hard. We get so wrapped up in the effort and the result that we fail to perform in the moment.

The fourth approach is the approach to go for. It's what sports psychologists call the challenge-response. We stay in the moment and see everything not as a problem but as a challenge to be overcome. Choose this one. When you can do this, you are able to present and work through whatever the challenges are. You aren't wrapped up in the result, and you are confident that you are giving your best under the circumstances. Often, you will gain a deeper rapport with your audience when you address the issue appropriately.

But what practical action should you take?

"The computer crashed, black screen of death crashed during my presentation. I had it memorized, so I carried on. Before that, the AV specialist loaded the wrong presentation; switched it myself and moved right along. Like our customer service, the quality of our presentation is best proven by the way we handle the hiccups, not a perfectly smooth experience. Who hasn't had audio issues?!"

— John D. Hanson

KEEP PEDALING

Eddie Van Halen gives some sage advice on how to handle mistakes. The lead guitarist of one of the greatest rock bands grew up in Holland with brother Alex. He once asked his dad (who was an accomplished classical musician) what to do when he made a mistake while playing music. His dad said in Dutch, "Gewoon door fietsen." That translates to "Just keep pedaling through."

Trivia: There are more bicycles than residents in the Netherlands. In cities like Amsterdam and The Hague up to 70 percent of all journeys are made by bike.

His dad went further, "Don't stop and let the audience know you've made a mistake . . . or [else] smile and do it twice. Then people will think you meant it."

Hat tip to Dr. Vincent Schmidt for sharing this piece of advice. Eddie recalled it back in 2012 as part of *Esquire* magazine's 80th birthday celebration.[36]

It's such a relevant piece of advice when presenting. You will never give a perfect speech. Dale Carnegie famously said there are three types of talks:

1. The one you practiced.

2. The one you gave.

3. And the one you wished you gave.

---

36. https://www.youtube.com/watch?v=wn9uHNcd3fY

The audience only gets to experience the second one. Make it the best you can.

TIP #30 - You are going to face the unexpected. Don't get hung up when you do. Keep pedaling.

3F FRAMEWORK

You have three options when something unexpected happens to keep the show moving:

1. FIX IT - For items you can solve, there is an obvious and simple solution. Fix the problem/issue. If your throat is scratchy, take a drink. (You DID bring water, didn't you!?) If the slide is incorrect, go to the correct one. If you drop your pen, pick it up. You might need to enlist someone else to solve the problem. (Would you get some paper towels for me please?)

2. FEATURE IT - Sometimes, it's best to address the issue by making everyone aware of it. Self-deprecating humor might be a way to address this. But be careful that you do not draw attention to something other than your message unless you've already seen the audience's attention derailed. Many issues that speakers feature are better left alone. But when everyone notices the problem, it's worth mentioning. The computer power going out. The group next door singing too loudly to ignore. The fire alarm going off.

3. FORGET IT - The hardest option in handling an issue is to let it go. Don't say a word. Don't attempt to address it. Just let it go. Because it's hard, you won't see a lot of this, and it's a great way to separate yourself from your competition. The splitting headache. The fly buzzing around your head. The fact that this is the first time you've presented this material. And your nerves. Each of these issues affects only the presenter and should just be forgotten.

The real problem is that you have to decide what to do in a fraction of a second. You don't have time to pull out your *Silver Goldfish* copy and hunt for this section. So, here's an easy checklist:

- If you can fix it, fix it. And be done. Skip to end.

- If you CAN'T fix it, then you've taken that off the table. Stop trying.

- Now ask, "Does this affect my ENTIRE audience?" Does everyone know about the problem? If yes, then feature it. Bring it up and acknowledge it. If no (it doesn't affect EVERYONE), then let it go. It's not an issue worth your trouble or the audience's attention.

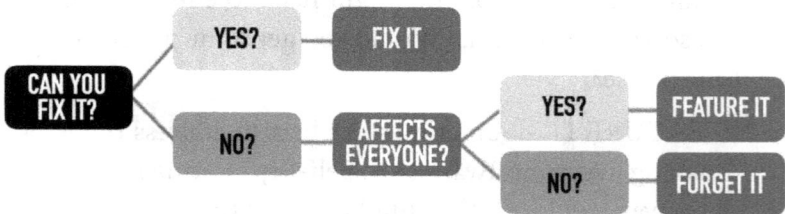

TIP #31 - When that moment of "Oh, heck!" hits you on stage, remember the fix it, feature it, and forget it options. And maybe include the fourth F. Just F it. Find someone to blame. Kidding of course.

The net result of handling these logistical issues is that it is easier to retain proper audience attention. When you make it easier for your audience to stay focused, you look smooth, prepared, and PROFESSIONAL. You appear to have been here before, cool, calm, and collected. And the audience will appreciate the effort you've made to make it easier to follow the talk you're giving. It's worth the effort to facilitate well .

Next we'll address how to entertain.

CHAPTER 10

ENTERTAIN

"I would rather entertain and hope that people learned something than educate people and hope they were entertained."

— Walt Disney

You've made a strong impression, connected with the audience, expressed yourself, and facilitated the elements. The last principle in being Loud enough to be heard is to maintain the attention of the audience and keep them entertained. The definition of entertain, according to Webster, is to hold the attention of agreeably, to admit into the mind; consider. That's the real goal of a presenter—to get the audience to consider their points and claims.

BRAIN RULES

If keeping the attention of the audience when speaking was a test, then 80 percent of presenters would fail. This stat is from Dr. John Medina and his groundbreaking book *Brain Rules*. So, how do you keep the audience engaged when presenting?

You need to understand the 10-minute rule of audience engagement. Here's an explanation from American Express:[37]

> "It is a well-known fact that attention wanes after about 10 minutes. However, most presenters seem to forget this and continue to drone on for an hour or more; they move from mind-numbing slide to slide, unaware of the painful effect on the audience. When you create your presentation, plan to have a strategic change every 10 minutes."

Here are nine solutions to reset your audience at least every 10 minutes:

1. Asking a pointed question to the audience

2. Show a short and pertinent video clip

3. Tell a relevant story or anecdote

---

37. https://www.americanexpress.com/en-us/business/trends-and-insights/articles/how-to-keep-your-audience-focused-on-your-presentation/

4. Get the group doing an exercise

5. Use a different medium (prop, whiteboard, flipchart)

6. Change where you speak by using the entire room

7. Get the audience to stand up and pair up for an exercise

8. Use a creative or funny GIF

9. Do your Q&A before you close the presentation

TIP #32 - It doesn't matter how amazing a presenter you are, you have to mix it up. The same approach will develop disinterest, and folks will biologically be forced to tune you out. To quote fellow speaker Jay Baer, "Same is lame." Variety is not only the spice of life but of presentations as well.

"I think it helps speakers to think more in terms of talking with their audience rather than talking at them. Gone are the days of people being willing to sit passively and have you pour information on them like a blanket that puts them to sleep. First rule is always, know your audience. Then you can select the methods and media that will help them most. And yes, absolutely include ways for them to participate with you, others in the audience, or some of the content. Get them doing something."

— Valerie Oleinik

ONE MORE THING

What can Steve Jobs teach us about presentation skills? The answer is plenty. In fact, Carmine Gallo wrote an entire book that breaks down lessons from the man. One is a simple fact that Jobs was not born a great presenter. Neither was Bill Gates or Barack Obama. They all worked on their presentation skills and improved over time.

There is one practice in particular that Steve Jobs used that warms our hearts. It is in the spirit of lagniappe, a little something extra that's thrown in for good measure.

At the end of each one of his Apple keynote presentations, Jobs would feign that he was finished and then with a glint in his eye announce, "One more thing . . ." The words would show up on a slide and the crowd would erupt.

Ewan Spence recalls one instance in *Forbes*:

> In September 2006, Jobs introduced the ability to purchase and download movies through iTunes. And then followed that with one more thing in the form of iTV (soon to be renamed Apple TV). And then Jobs followed that one more thing with one more one more thing, and John Mayer made his customary Easter egg appearance not as cover art, or a ringtone, but live onstage singing *Waiting For The World To Change*.[38]

YOU ARE NOT SKYWALKER

In Donald Miller's book *Building a StoryBrand*, he states, "To enter into our customer's story, we should play the role of guide." The fatal mistake that both brands and presenters make is positioning themselves as the hero in a story instead of the guide. That's a recipe for failure. The presenter must be focused on the hero (the audience member).[39]

---

38. https://www.forbes.com/sites/ewanspence/2013/10/19/five-of-the-greatest-one-more-thing-moments-from-steve-jobs-and-apple/#4df60d9f7169

39. https://www.millerheimangroup.com/resources/blog/how-to-tell-your-customers-story-hint-youre-not-the-hero/

TIP #33 - Be the guide. In movies and stories, the guide, not the hero, is the one with the most authority. Be like Gandalf and Yoda.

HUMOR

Humor is intensely personal. It's also incredibly connective. But if it sends the wrong message, it can undermine the real message. Avoid jokes that anyone could tell. Personal stories and self-deprecating humor that connects you with humanity are usually safe. Never make a subgroup the butt of a joke.

TIP #34 - When in doubt, leave it out is a good mantra to live by in the humor department.

> "I make sure to always customize to their language as much as possible, create humor to their industry when I can, and act as the biggest cheerleader for those making the event happen—from the stage—it floors the person usually."
>
> — Jason Hewlett, CSP, CPAE

We've examined the five key elements of being LOUD and heard above distractions. We examined Impress, Connect, Express, Facilitate, and Entertain. Next we'll examine the five key elements of CLEAR.

CHAPTER 11

OBJECTIVE

"In whatever position you find yourself, first determine your objective."

— Ferdinand Foch

We've shown how you can be Loud—heard above the noise in your audience's head. There are many distractions to overcome; there is much we can do as presenters to help our audience focus and be mentally involved in our journey. This includes our behavior, handling the environment, and finding ways to present and entertain, in the strictest sense of the words.

But we must eventually get to the point. That's where clarity comes in. Our content must be delivered in such a way that the audience walks away with something they did not arrive with. We now turn our attention to CLEAR—the second half of the Signal Corps creed. The ability to be understood.

Alan played basketball in high school. During one game, his coach called out a play as the half wound toward conclusion. The play was called "Pan Am." The point guard, in the middle of the game with an opposing defender hounding him, heard the call, stopped his dribble, turned to ref and began screaming, "Time out! Time out!" The referee granted his request. As the team gathered around Coach, he had the most confused look on his face, and his words were not kind. "What are you doing? Why didn't you run Pan Am?" The point guard sheepishly replied, "I heard 'Time Out.'"

Coach did not have a problem with being loud. Everyone in the gym heard him calling the play. But he was not clear. And when we are not clear as presenters, the wrong message is delivered, the wrong action is executed, and the wrong outcome is realized.

OVERSTUFFING

Probably the greatest problem with clarity in business presentations is the tendency to try to put too much into the presentation. Alan will often ask coaching clients, "How long did it take you to learn what you know?" The answer is usually years and sometimes even decades. How then could you expect to share all of that information in a nice compact 50-minute presentation?

TIP #35 - We need to release ourselves of the obligation to cover everything we know. Figure out what is important to the audience. Find out your reason for being on that stage giving that presentation.

MOST IMPORTANT PERSON IN THE ROOM

Have you ever known someone who thinks they know it all? We seriously doubt that this is you if you're reading this book. And you certainly wouldn't still be reading if you did. The problem with these "know-it-all" types is that they fail to see the most important person in the room. We call it Rule #1. It's the simple truth that the presentation is not about you, the presenter. It can be difficult to convince yourself of that. After all, it's YOUR name on the conference program. It's YOUR content that was developed for the update. It's YOUR expertise on the line for a sales presentation. But in each case as presenters, we should quickly conclude that the audience or client is the real reason we're there.

Rule #1: It's not about you.

TIP #36 - Make your presentation about the audience, not yourself.

PURPOSE

Which leads to you creating the purpose for your presentation. Why are you speaking? What should happen as a result? Let's call these objectives. It's a semantic point, but please avoid the word "agenda." An agenda is an order of talking points. And in meetings or presentations, it only takes one expert and one extrovert (heaven help us if it's the same person), and we'll never be done talking. We can never be done with an agenda.

TIP #37 - Have an objective for your presentation and keep it tangible and measurable.

We had a very successful salesman in one of our workshops. He claimed his objective was to get a signature on the contract. Since the product he was selling was priced in the millions of dollars, Alan knew this was not a trivial sales call or a short cycle. He asked, *"Is the person who can authorize that amount of expense in the room?"* The answer was quick and short: *"No."* Alan advised, *"Then you can't ask for a signature on a contract as the objective of your presentation."* The salesman was indignant, defensive, and condescending in his next response. *"Well, you clearly don't know anything about sales. Our goal is to get commitment. I'll never see the CEO or CFO face-to-face in this business. It's just the way things work."* And he crossed his arms, huffed loudly, and disengaged for the rest of the class, no doubt dreaming of the commission check that one signature would give him. But his goal wasn't attainable. It was quite measurable, but not attainable. For a presentation objective, "getting a signature" would cause him to say and cover things that would be frustrating for a person in the audience without signature authority.

CREATE POWERFUL OBJECTIVES

What then, does our audience need to hear, want to hear, and need direction for?

Here are some presentation objectives that are weak and unmeasurable (all lifted from client conversations):

- Provide an overview
- Discuss
- Review
- Update
- Give an overview
- Talk about
- Introduce
- Present about
- Take questions
- Wrap up
- Offer feedback
- Go through
- Explain
- Go through PowerPoint

The last one (Go through PowerPoint) actually is quite measurable. PowerPoint tells you after the last slide, "End of Slide Show." But if that's your only goal—to get through your presentation—you've certainly shortchanged your audience and missed an opportunity.

Can you imagine the signers of the Declaration of Independence making "Discuss our options" as their meeting goal? Or Abraham

Lincoln suggesting "to review the situation" at Gettysburg? Or Martin Luther King Jr. proposing "I'd like to explain a few thoughts on racial equality"? Or JFK presenting to Congress, "Let's go through some aspects of the space program"? They all had a greater objective. They wanted to win over the minds of their audience and get them to ACT. That should be our goal every time we present.

Nick Morgan says in the book *Give Your Speech, Change the World: How To Move Your Audience to Action*, "The only reason to give a speech is to change the world. An old friend of mine, a speechwriter, used to say that to me. He meant it as a challenge. It was his way of saying that if you're going to take all the trouble to prepare and deliver a speech, make it worthwhile. Change the world."

TIP #38 - Create a strong objective. Here are some possible objectives you might consider to change the world of your audience:

- Change their behavior
- Sign up for your newsletter
- Sign the contract (assuming the signer is in your audience)
- Do their own research
- Buy your book or coaching program
- Take a test drive
- Try the product for 30 days
- Tell someone about what you've experienced

The objective must be based on what your audience is prepared to do. If they've never heard of your product, then getting them to sign a contract is probably not feasible. Conversely, if they've done business with you for two decades, covering your corporate office locations is boring and misses the mark. Understanding your audience as completely as possible is the quickest way to creating content they will enjoy, remember, and act on.

ASK QUESTIONS

It's not easy work understanding your audience. It involves thought, research, iteration, and empathy. Empathy! Feelings! That's the place to start. Put yourself in the shoes of your audience. What was it like before you knew what you know now? What's it like to listen to the last speaker of the day after sitting in a conference all day?

Here are some questions to get you started:

- What do they HAVE to know (perhaps what they asked you to cover)?

- What do they NEED to know (to act on the objective you've uncovered)?

- What do they ALREADY know (which you can use to engage, ask for involvement to help others in the room, or skip altogether)?

- What process do they go through to come to decisions?

TIP #39 - Create objectives and come up with good content based on those objectives by asking questions. Lots of questions.

ITERATION

When working on your presentation, you can almost never get your content right in a single pass. Let it sit. Come back to it. Try again tomorrow. Iteration may be the most underestimated pre-sentation development skill out there. Last-minute presentation development, especially when you rely on past material, will most assuredly result in missing the mark with your audience. Your past material may have been a perfect fit at the original delivery, but don't assume what fit then will fit now. Research relentlessly.

TIP #40 - Make multiple passes and iterate.

You now understand the objective of your presentation. Next let's tackle the importance of simplification.

CHAPTER 12

SIMPLIFY

"Make everything as simple as possible, and no simpler.

— Albert Einstein"

We're examining the way to make our content Clear—able to be understood (and hopefully repeated) by our audience. We have an objective. We know what we want to happen as a result of our presentation. But how can we present decades worth of expertise to a crowd that may not fully be at our level of understanding and experience?

The first step in helping your audience understand is to figure out your "One Thing." It's hard. There's no better explanation than from cowboy mentor Curly (Jack Palance) advising mid-life crisis Mitch (Billy Crystal) in the movie *City Slickers*.

> Curly: You know what the secret of life is?
>
> Mitch: No, what?
>
> Curly: (holds up his leather-gloved hand with index finger pointed up) This.
>
> Mitch: Your finger?
>
> Curly: One thing, just one thing.
>
> Mitch: That's great, but what's the one thing?
>
> Curly: That's what you've got to figure out.

Before you start making your slides pretty, before you design your audience interaction, before you plan your Big Entrance, before you brainstorm objections, you need to figure out what you want to say in ONE sentence. That's the first question Alan asks anyone wanting help in their messaging. After asking hundreds of people the question, only one person has ever been able to do it on the first try. When Alan asked Stan the question, Stan shared that the Goldfish series message is centered around one simple phrase: "Little things make a big difference." With *Silver Goldfish*, the series is now 13 books deep. But the "One Thing" has not changed. It's that kind of clarity that keeps audiences listening and coming back for more.

It's not going to be easy. Your One Thing may be hard to discover. Mitch needed two weeks on a horse to find his. You probably don't need a horse, but you do need to spend some time to find your One Thing.

Here are some "One Thing" sentences from client presentations we've coached:

- Walnut Grove was a great place to grow up. (50-year reunion speech)
- Your perfect life does not exist (yet). (creativity expert)
- Self-care isn't selfish. (stress management expert)
- You can define what you become. (given by a quadriplegic)
- Solving member problems is the ticket to growth. (Association consultant)
- The devil's in the details. (CPA)

TIP #41 - Find the "One Thing" for your presentation.

CURSE OF KNOWLEDGE

Dan and Chip Heath write in their seminal work on communication, *Made to Stick*, that a presenter is afflicted with the Curse of Knowledge (you simply MUST say this with a slow, reverberating, macabre voice). Once you have learned something, you cannot remember what it was like not to know it. Imagine looking at text in your native language and not automatically reading it. (This is a key principle in visuals as we will see later.) Try to think about being on your hands and knees and not knowing how to get up. You had that situation in early life! Consider seeing 2 + 2 = ? and not immediately knowing it was four. But presenters appear to forget about this Curse of Knowledge all too frequently when creating their presentations.

Alan was a TA (teacher's assistant) for a freshman calculus class in graduate school. He can remember one day early in the semester the professor was asked a question from a very eager freshman on the front row. The student was clearly confused, wanted badly to understand this key point, and had risked the potential damage to his image to ask a question in front of 120 peers. By Alan's recollection, this was class three or four, so it was probably something about limits or expanding a difference quotient. Nothing earth-shatteringly difficult for a decent math student, but easy concepts often do not start easy, and this student needed clarification. The professor's response is memorable decades later. He stopped dead in his tracks and with a very pained look on his face said, "Well, I think it's painfully obvious." And without answering the question, he furrowed his brow, turned back to the chalkboard (Alan just dated himself), and returned to his lecture. The poor student didn't ask another question all semester. This very intelligent math professor (and usually very good instructor) could not remember what it was like not to do simple, foundational math.

This scenario is played out daily in the business world. Your audience doesn't know all the acronyms you use (but they probably won't stop you to ask). They don't know what that statistic means. They probably don't know all the names you drop and their position on the organizational chart either.

Recently, Alan was coaching a presenter team for a $20 million sales pitch. Since the domain was not one he was familiar with (a very technical and politically-sensitive project in a foreign country), Alan was constantly trying to understand what they were talking about even as he advised them on their presentation. The solicitation had used the phrase "conflict-sensitive" and one presenter was going on at length about what that meant for the presentation. Alan reread the paper and still didn't understand, so he stopped her and asked, "What, exactly, is meant by the phrase 'conflict-sensitive'?" There was a long pause and finally three of the other team members sheepishly confessed, "I wondered that, too." Apparently if Alan hadn't asked, they were prepared to play along and pretend they knew what was wanted and expected. Turns out, the apparent expert also didn't know, and that resulted in a sidebar conversation about what was wanted by the bid judges, which led to clarity on what was needed in the presentation.

TIP #42 - Do not assume your audience knows anything. Use research and testing to find out. Clarity begins with knowing what matters.

SIMPLIFY YOUR MESSAGE

There are three ways you can simplify your message to aid in its digestion by your audience.

1. THE WORDS YOU USE

Every discipline has lingo. Every culture uses phrases that only matter to them. The warning to presenters is that people outside your bubble are in your audience too.

Alan grew up in a medical household. Every other member of his immediate family is either a doctor or a nurse. As a small child, he can remember playing on the floor one day and jumping up to his feet. The world began to spin and he staggered to the floral print couch under the picture window in the living room. Alan cried out to his dad, sitting in his black naugahyde recliner reading a journal. Barely lifting an eye, his dad shared, "You're experiencing autonomic instability related to orthostatic induction." Alan thought his dad had lost his mind. Never one to back down in a discussion, he offered, "No, I'm pretty sure I just stood up too fast." Alan's father replied, "That's what I said." But he didn't say it in a language a non-medical person could understand.

Alan took his daughter to overnight camp one spring. She wanted to shoot the BB guns. Sounded like a splendid idea and beat making mud pies in the sand. Upon arrival at the shooting facility, there was a line. During the wait in line, the supervisor/instructor was giving a briefing on BB gun safety. Virtually everyone in America knows the danger of BB guns thanks to the movie *A Christmas Story*. "*You'll shoot your eye out!*" We can imagine structuring the safety briefing with three points:

1. Wear glasses
2. Point the gun THAT way (pointing to the range)
3. Stop shooting when we say "STOP"

Continued . . .

Should take 20 seconds. But this supervisor/instructor was (he said) a nationally certified BB gun instructor. He covered the structure of the gun, its performance (in FPS, feet-per-second), its function, the effect of wind and ricochets, what could malfunction, alternate ammunitions, comparison to higher grade air rifles, and . . . . We slept through the end. Young daughters were all asking, "When are we going to get to shoot?" It was the only question anyone in the audience had.

There is only one way to combat the Curse of Knowledge and use language your audience understands. That is to ask an audience that doesn't know what you know. Alan's corporate pilot brother-in-law asked his 11-year-old daughter to read his performance review before asking his boss for a raise. When she didn't understand half of what he'd written, he eliminated that content, because his boss didn't know aviation either. The resulting simple half page got him the raise he asked for with no discussion.

TIP #43 - Use common words that your audience understands. If you have a choice between a pretentious word that makes you sound smart and a simpler word, choose the simpler word. Allow your audience to follow your train of thought. When you speak simply, your audience understands, follows, and can more easily remember what you said. If the audience has to work hard to understand, then your message isn't likely to stick.

If your words are only known inside your group or organization, then your message will only be effective inside your group or organization. Be careful of acronyms, unique language, or inside jokes when presenting to an outside group.

2. THE LENGTH OF YOUR MESSAGE

When you know a lot, it's hard to say a little. This has far-reaching effects on your audience. They simply cannot digest everything you have to say. Your college classes were spread over 16 weeks. Every educator knows there is a limit to the capacity of the human mind. The mind cannot absorb what the butt cannot endure. Research[40] suggests you can only process four short-term memory items at a time. You must find a way to store them in long-term memory or they will be lost. Likewise any new material cannot be processed and maintained. It too will be "lost."

TIP #44 - The way to manage a presentation's timing is not to talk faster or cram more onto a single slide. The method that works best is to figure out what you need to convey. Get each section of your presentation down to that One Thing. Then and only then are you ready to add detail to support or illustrate your One Thing points within the time you will have.

I watched a lunch-and-learn one time where the group was highly entertaining. They gave out prizes, had a recorded

Continued . . .

---

40. https://www.ncbi.nlm.nih.gov/pubmed/11515286

rap song, showed pictures of their process, and generally had the audience in the palm of their hands. That is until Time ran out and people began to leave and return to work. I'll never forget their closing statement, a sad testimony to their preparation and time management. One of them said, "Well, it looks like we're out of time. We didn't get to the next part, which was the real point of the presentation. If you want to hear it, I guess you can come up and talk to us." WHAT?! You showed a homemade rap video but ran out of time to give your key point? What a waste of my time! What a lost opportunity!

I had a student give a four-minute and thirty second story as an intro to their midterm dry run once. I stopped him and reminded him the entire presentation had to be under five minutes. His response was, "But this is a GREAT story!" I couldn't disagree. It was a great story. But it simply could not be used in that time frame. Find something else. End on time.

— Alan Hoffler

3. FIND SPECIFIC EXAMPLES

This has become a go-to piece of advice when Alan coaches speakers. In his experience, there isn't anything that will entertain and engage an audience more than being specific.

Presenters love to use generic phrases. We need to find solutions. This is a big deal. I'm sure you're all facing issues in your life. The problem is that the generic doesn't cause the brain to exclaim, "Hey, he's talking to me!" By adding a specific reference, the brain makes the connection. It pictures a real-life instance that matters to them.

If you find yourself uttering a generic phrase (usually indicated by words like thing, stuff, issue, problem, or non-specific amounts), tack on a clause and add one or two examples to illustrate the generic.

"We need to find solutions, like how we can find mistakes earlier and fix them before we ship the product."

"This is a big deal. Getting this right means the difference between going public and going broke."

"You're facing issues in your life. Maybe it's financial stress. Perhaps you have a child who is struggling or you're genuinely concerned about your parents' health."

Alan used this technique with an audience once that looked a lot like him, demographically speaking. After he spoke, a guy came up to him and said, "I loved your talk. Especially the stories." Then he paused and cautiously confessed, perhaps realizing as he spoke that it might condemn his listening skills, "But when you were talking about your kids, I was thinking about my kids." He never realized that's exactly why Alan told those stories. He wanted the audience to think about their own kids, to be engaged in the topic through the filter of their own life.

Being specific is entertaining. It captures the mind and thought and consideration of your audience. Generic references don't do that.

TIP #45 - The specific is always more powerful than the generic.

Implementing these three tips to simplify your message will make your message stick, help your audience remember you for all the right reasons, and keep their minds engaged while you speak. When coupled with a clear objective and fine-tuned core message, this makes a great presentation for a particular audience.

SPEAKING TO A MIXED AUDIENCE

Almost no audience is demographically or experientially uniform. There will be differences in age, culture, beliefs, knowledge, and attitude. For instance, you may be presenting a very technical concept, but the audience includes engineers (who love the technical details), business leaders (who are more concerned with the big picture economic impact), and support personnel (who want to know about systems and risk, but don't know or want technical details). What do you do when you have a varied audience?

Usually when we ask this question, people say, "Speak to the largest group" or "Find middle ground." But this has dangers that could sink your message. If you water down your content and aim for the middle ground, you could miss the extremes of both the highly technical and the big picture thinkers. If you speak to the majority, you very likely will miss messaging the decision-maker. What to do?

This is a slippery slope that requires careful thought and strategy. As always, strive for the SIMPLE answer.

SOLUTION ONE: SEPARATE THE GROUP

When possible, it's best to separate different groups. Elementary school teachers know this. They inherit students who are reading above grade level on day one, kids who are at grade level, and kids who don't yet know their alphabet. How do you structure a reading lesson? Divide the children into "reading groups"—the Bears, the Lions, and the Zebras—to teach each at the level best for them. Likewise separating the intended audience into separate groups lets you speak directly and appropriately to each group's needs. But it's rarely possible to separate an audience this way in the business world.

SOLUTION TWO: PICK ONLY ONE GROUP

This is almost always one of the suggestions, and it's valid. But you need to pick the right group, not the most populous one or the one most like you. When pitching to a small business, speak to the decision maker. It may be your only opportunity to do so. When giving a technical update, you must talk technical. If you're speaking at a conference, match your talk to your abstract. You're almost sure to get some folks who misidentified themselves, but you'll lose more if you advertise an "advanced" seminar and spend half the time "catching people up to speed."

SOLUTION THREE: LET THE GROUP HELP YOU PRESENT

This is the hardest but potentially most rewarding method. Find a way to get the group involved. It could be as simple as having them answer questions. It may be using exercises or group activities. But if there's a wide variety of knowledge, tapping into that knowledge can be key in keeping everyone engaged. The experts will often be delighted to share their expertise and the newbie will appreciate not being left behind. It's a risk because you're giving up control, but the reward is great. You gain an engaged audience that is actively participating in the presentation and outcome.

At this point, we understand our objective and have simplified our message. Now it's time to put the framework of our presentation together. That begins with outlining.

CHAPTER 13

OUTLINE

*"All you need is the plan, the road map, and the
courage to press on to your destination."*

—Earl Nightingale

Wnat's the first thing you do when preparing to create a presentation? Fire up PowerPoint? No! The first thing you do is assess how much time you have for preparing for the presentation.

I know fellow speakers such as Tom Triumph who've spent hundreds of hours getting ready for a 15-minute TED Talk. That said, you can also spend an hour prepping for a 45-minute presentation.

Once you figure out the time you can dedicate to prep, then you should be thinking about what Nancy Duarte calls the "Rule of Thirds" in her book *slide:ology*.[41] The Rule of Thirds is a simple framework for maximizing your time. Here's how it works.

THE FIRST THIRD

The first third of outlining your presentation is spent collecting and organizing. We encourage you to take an analog approach of sketching. This is a time of exploration. It includes understanding your audience and coming up with your One Thing. But it needs some structure. An outline.

While outlining, here is a list of some of the questions to consider:

- What's the issue or concern? The your goal is to draw attention to what matters for your audience. According to Kathy McAfee and Leesa Wallace in the book *Sharpening Your Point*, there are only three things your audience wants to know: 1. Why am I here? 2. What do you want me to do? 3. Why should I?

- Where are my breaks to reset the audience? As we shared in chapter 10, if your presentation is going to be more than 10 minutes long, you need to plan for resetting. That requires strategic placement of elements such as exercises, video, and Q&A.

---

41. https://www.coreography.com/how-much-time-should-i-spend-creating-my-presentation/

- What's my opening? Is there a specific story or a statistic that will grab the attention of the audience and set the context for the presentation?

- What's my close? How will I pull it all together and finish the presentation? What's my call to action for the audience?

TIP #46 - Go analog to create your outline in your first third. Try using colored Post-it notes and a Sharpie. Post-it notes allow you to move things around very easily. The size of the note and the Sharpie will force you to keep your thoughts and ideas on the big picture.

THE SECOND THIRD

The middle third of your time is spent designing your visuals. We'll spend the next chapter on visualizing your presentation. But for the purpose of preparing your presentation, here are some questions you should be asking:

- Does this talk require slides?

- Which tool will I use? (PowerPoint, Keynote, Prezi, whiteboard, etc.)

- Can I use props?

- What's the point I'm trying to illustrate?

- What's the best way to make that point visually?

- Do I have the skills to make the visuals, or should I enlist help?

TIP #47 - If you are creating slides, be sure to use high-resolution images and limit the text on each slide.

THE FINAL THIRD

The final third of your time is spent practicing and rehearsing your presentation. Warning: this can be painful and that's why most people avoid it. Don't fall victim to not putting in the time. Take a cue from the rule of thumb in theater. Actors will rehearse one hour for every minute of the play. Speaking coach Stephanie Scotti advises that you should rehearse your presentation at least five times. She reasons that only after the fifth time will you start to feel comfortable. This comfort level allows you to get out of your head and be more present with the audience when presenting.

TIP #48 - Rehearse out loud and try to mimic your actual setting for the presentation. For example, are you standing or sitting? A rehearsal is often a full presentation from beginning to end. This is important from a timing perspective, but it's also advisable to practice delivery. Practice allows you to work on shorter sections of your presentation. Focus on practicing the beginning and ending. Don't forget the old New York City joke. A tourist stops a New Yorker on the street and asks, "Excuse me, how do you get to Carnegie Hall?" The New Yorker thinks for a second and responds, "Practice, practice, practice."

"I spend hours rehearsing. I was recently advised to put my sticky notes high up on a wall instead of on a surface. Apparently, looking up at your notes helps you recall better than looking down. Who knew?"

— Sara Canaday

THREE IS THE MAGIC NUMBER

When building a presentation from the ground up, it's important not to overshare. Don't try to compress everything you know into the presentation. How many points should you share? Is one too little and five too many? Well, if you grew up with the television show *Schoolhouse Rock*, you'd know there is a magic number. Yes there is—it's three. Three is the magic number. And when it comes to presenting, it's even more important. If the goal when speaking is to be remember-able, then you need to take advantage of this powerful heuristic.

A heuristic is defined as "any approach to problem-solving, learning, or discovery that employs a practical method not guaranteed to be optimal or perfect, but sufficient for the immediate goals."[42]

If the goal is to be remember-able, people remember things in threes. Your audience is more likely to consume and absorb the ideas or concepts presented to them when they are grouped into sets of three.

In the words of Carmine Gallo, "Great speeches are often divided into three themes, plays are often divided into three acts, and the same technique applies to persuasive presentations."

From the *Schoolhouse Rock* song:

> Every triangle has three sides
> No more, no less, you don't have to guess
> When it's three, you can see
> It's a magic number

And that's the truth, the whole truth, and nothing but the truth.

---

42. https://www.101computing.net/heuristic-approaches-to-problem-solving/

TIP #49 - Go forward and implement the power of three in your presentations. Veni, vidi, vici!

BALANCE

When outlining your presentation, remember to balance your points. Don't go through the first point in 25 minutes, then touch on the remaining points in the last five minutes. Try to make your points equal. If there's something more important, say so.

TIP #50 - Balance out your points.

Abraham Lincoln structured many of his speeches with the past, the present, and the future. Consider his Gettysburg Address:

- Four score and seven years ago . . .
- Now we are engaged . . .
- The world will little note, nor long remember . . .

STRUCTURE

Here are nine possible ways to structure your content when putting together a presentation:

- Acronym / Mnemonic
- Time / Chronology
- Order
- Position
- Rank

- Alliteration

- Questions (Who-what-when-where-why-how)

- Pro / Con

- Catchy phrases

TIP #51 - Use a structure—any structure—when outlining.

> "When presenting in an instructional classroom environment, I use the 20/20/20 rule which is dividing an hour into three roughly equal sections. Take 20 minutes to introduce the topic and set up the associated activity, 20 minutes for students to apply the concept in an active group exercise, and finally 20 minutes to debrief on the activity and summarize the learning."
>
> — Karl Sharicz

We've determined our "One Thing," created a structure to hold all our content, and have allotted the time we have for each part. Now we can focus on how to create the greatest impact possible. It's time to focus on how to best visualize your content.

CHAPTER 14

VISUALIZE

"If I really believe that visual representation and narrative are ways to convey important, complex ideas, and if the world is gravitating toward this form, then geez, I better do it myself. I want to do it myself."

— Daniel H. Pink

You've understood your objective and boiled it down to your core message. The outline has been completed. Once we have our message clear, we can ask, "What's the best way to make this memorable?" The answer will frequently involve visuals. These visuals can take the shape of slides, whiteboards, flipcharts, or props. If the presentation requires visuals, this chapter will provide you with the tips on how to create a dynamic visual presentation.

Let's start with the tool that supports the overwhelming majority of presentations.

It was originally called Presenter. Launched by Apple in 1987, the program was black and white only at first. Robert Gaskins had invented the program three years earlier. It solved a big problem. Most presentations were done with transparencies and an overhead projector. The program eliminated the need to manually re-type content on the transparencies. Two days after Presenter's release all 8,000 copies on floppy disks had been sold.

Unfortunately, a New Jersey company had already trademarked the name Presenter. Gaskins thought up a new name while in the shower: PowerPoint.

Interesting name, but what is a power point? The concept comes from photography. The camera viewfinder is often divided like a tic-tac-toe grid. This creates nine equally sized boxes. The four points where the lines of the grid intersect are called power points. The goal is to place your center of interest on one of the four power points.

This leads us to our first important TIP in slide design.

TIP #52 - Use the four power points. First, use them when placing the focus of the image. Second, use the power points as a reference on where you place text on the slide.

IMAGES

Should you use images when you present? Stan uses copious images when he delivers keynotes and workshops. Fellow speaker Todd Dewett uses zero. Is there one correct way? Alan sits somewhere in the middle and uses a combination of text and photos when he presents. As with most things in life, it way depends.

Why use images? The single biggest reason is memorability. When you present, the goal should be that your message comes across "Loud" and "Clear" for your audience. Is the message shared in a way that's remember-able? It depends on the person and the visual, but our ability to recall a message is enhanced by up to 650 percent when we use visuals. Why such a big bump? It's because of a phenomenon called the Picture Superiority Effect.[43]

---

43. https://en.wikipedia.org/wiki/Picture_superiority_effect

The picture superiority effect refers to the fact that pictures and images are more likely to be remembered than words alone.

Hear something—three days later recall is 10 percent.

Hear something and add image—three days later recall is upward of 65 percent.

TIP #53 - Should you use images when present? It depends on your type of presentation, but using images can enhance your audience's ability to remember your message or call to action.

TEXT

As we just learned with the Picture Superiority Effect, images can aid memory of the spoken word. A high percentage of the time in corporate presenting, the use of images translate into slides. And those highly effective visuals can derail a presentation with the overuse of one thing—bullets. This one element can derail and kill your presentation. There is a saying about presentations. Let me bullet it out for you:

- Guns do not
- Kill presentations
- Bullets do

This saying is an adaptation of a famous quote. In 1993, Senator Daniel Patrick Moynihan of New York proposed a huge tax increase on the most vicious types of ammunition, pointing out that, unlike guns, ammunition doesn't last forever. "Guns don't kill people," Moynihan said, "bullets do."

Let's examine the four biggest bullet mistakes:

1. The simplest mistake is overusing bullets in your slides.
2. If you use them, don't make the mistake of bringing them in all at once. Because while you are speaking to the first bullet, the audience is already reading ahead and ignoring you.

3. Reading your bullets word for word is also a mistake. Don't insult the intelligence of your audience. On average, they can read four times faster than you speak. If you put a sentence on your slide, you (and everyone in your audience) will read it. The only time that might be useful is for an audience trying to digest their second language. Otherwise, you're not a presenter, you're a narrator, and I suggest hiring James Earl Jones for the job. (No matter who you are, he has a better voice than you.)

4. Making the mistake of using full sentences with your bullets. Or, God forbid, multiple sentences. The one exception is when sharing a quote with multiple sentences.

Seth Godin wrote a blog post about how the tool of PowerPoint has been abused. He wrote, "If there was any other tool as widely misused in your organization, you'd ban it. The cost is enormous in lost opportunity and lost time."[44]

TIP #54 - Don't use bullets. If you do, keep the text to a minimum.

"When PowerPoint was first released 30 years ago I thought it was amazing. For a sales guy to be able to create visuals was so cool. However, I must confess that I had some slides in those early years with more copy than white space! Boy did I learn quickly that it is the perfect way to suck the energy out of a room."

— Dean Karrel

---

44. https://seths.blog/2010/04/powerpoint-makes-us-stupidthese-bullets-can-kill/

FONT CHOICE

Comic Sans is not funny. Neither is the default font for Power-Point—Calibri. The font you choose communicates. Don't use the default. Stand out in a sea of sameness when creating your slides. Avoid the default and heed the advice of Jay Baer, which we repeat here, "Same is lame."

Fonts matter. Don't use the default font. Pick a distinctive, easy to read font that adds a little personality to your slides. There are hundreds of options. Here are 15 suggestions:

1. Baskerville
2. Cantora One
3. Hobo Std
4. Gotham
5. Impact
6. Marker Felt
7. Montserrat
8. Open Sans
9. Oswald
10. Pacifico Regular
11. Proxima Nova
12. PT Sans Bold
13. Rokkitt
14. Ubuntu
15. Candara

What's the sans refer to Comic Sans? Sans is Old French for without. Without what? Laughs? No, the without is referring to serifs. Serifs are "little feet" or finishes on letters or numbers in certain fonts. [See ABC image below for example] One of the advantages of serif fonts is readability. Studies have found that serif typefaces are easier to read because the added strokes make each character more distinctive. More distinctive letters are easier for the eye to recognize quickly.[45]

abc   abc
Georgia, Serif   Helvetica, Sans-Serif

Photo Credit: Wikimedia Commons[46]

TIP #55 - Cast aside Calibri. Present sans Comic Sans. Pick a font that helps communicate your style and message. Rise above the sameness.

Other elements to consider for fonts are kerning and weights.

Kerning - Kerning is the spacing between letters, numbers, or symbols. This may impact readability.

Weight - Weight refers to the thickness of letters, numbers or symbols (normal, bold, extra bold, italic, narrow) Most fonts have options. Weight can add emphasis to the text.

45. https://www.figma.com/dictionary/serif/
46. https://commons.wikimedia.org/wiki/File:Textserifs.gif

"I sometimes even change the font color in my email responses, as well as the font. Sometimes those small, subtle changes make a difference in grabbing mindshare and attention."

— Waldo Waldman

It is a shame that most people use the defaults when firing up PowerPoint. The problem relates to what the program was born from. It replaced transparencies. Transparencies were laden with text and graphics; 55 percent of overheads contained bullets, 70 percent contained diagrams, and 35 percent combined both.

FONT PLACEMENT

You have picked a good font. You are limiting the words (and avoiding bullets). Now, where do you put words on a slide when presenting? Here are three things to consider:

1. HEADS UP. AVOID THE BOTTOM - Where not to put your words. Credit to slide guru Wendy Gates Corbett, MS, CPLP and CEO of Refresher Training LLC for this advice. Be mindful that text on the bottom-third of a slide may get cut off by people's heads. Don't put anything important on the bottom of the slide.

2. HEED THE POWER POINTS - As shared earlier, place your center of interest on one of the four power points. Remember, not only where you place the focus of the photo, but also where you place text on the slide.

3. UNDERSTAND CONTRAST - In the simplest terms, place light-colored text on a dark background and darker text on a light background.

TIP #56 - Use color of text and placement to maximize readability and impact.

FONT SIZE

What's the rule for font size when creating slides for a presentation? Ideally, you don't put words on your slides. You let the image communicate your message. But when you need to place words on your slides, how big should your font be?

If your slides are going to be displayed on a three-story screen at the side of the stage, the answer would be very different than if your display is your laptop at Panera Bread. Our preference is a minimum font size of 30. Two things should be considered:

1. Readability - Is the font size readable for the audience?

2. Audience - What's the age of the audience, how far are they from the screen, and how big is the screen?

TIP #57 - Former Apple evangelist, author, and speaker Guy Kawasaki has a rule of thumb that takes the guesswork out of font sizes.[47]

It's an equation:

Step 1: Determine the age of the oldest person in the audience. For example, age 65 (Guy's age)

Step 2: Divide their age by 2. 65 divided by 2 is 32.5. Round it up and 33 would be your minimum font size.

---

47. https://guykawasaki.com/the_102030_rule/

By the way, where does the phrase rule of thumb come from? In English, it refers to an approximate method for doing something based on practical experience rather than theory. The exact origin of the phrase is uncertain. The earliest appearance is from James Durham in 1685, "Many Christians are like to foolish builders, who build by guess, and by rule of thumb (as we use to speak), and not by Square and Rule."[48]

COLORS

Microsoft gives you 16.7 million colors to choose from. Please don't use that many. Usually you want to choose colors that are consistent with your company's brand. Your company may give you a template, which you should probably use. If you're choosing your own colors, pick colors that contrast. Black and white provide the highest contrast. But it might be a bit stark for presenters not named Steve Jobs. Black backgrounds have the advantage of not casting shadows if you happen to wander into the Tractor Beam. White backgrounds can help light the room if it's dark, and they are easier to read when using reflected light like from your projector. But lavender text on a fluorescent gold background will drive people to the eye doctor. It doesn't matter if they were the school colors of your high school. Make sure the colors you choose are generally appealing, comfortable to look at, and provide adequate contrast.

---

48. https://freakonomics.com/2011/07/01/rule-of-thumb/

One in every eight men has some level of color blindness. Don't rely solely on color to make a point.

TIP #58 - Pick high contrast, bold colors.

TRANSITION & BUILDS

"My advice is to keep it clean and simple. Avoid going overboard with content, special effects and too many images on a single slide."

— Dave Crenshaw

Flying objects are only interesting when there is an Unidentified in front of them. Just because some developer at Microsoft created the ability to fly your text around the screen, scroll it inside out, and have it explode does not mean it's a good technique to use. Animations take time, frequently resulting in a presenter "overclicking." They also can cause problems with slow machines, over the web, and with video. Unless movement is part of the message (for instance, showing data flow from the server to the client), drop the animation and just have your object/text "appear."

TIP #59 - Keep it simple and minimize animations.

In summary, for visualizing, use images, limit text, and put more power in PowerPoint. Now, let's examine timing when presenting.

CHAPTER 15

TIME

"Time is an illusion, timing is an art."

— Stefan Emunds

The last technique to make your message Clear is to manage time. This leads us to the only cardinal rule of presenting. When your time is up, you need to be done. Nothing is more egregious than stealing time.

THE CARDINAL RULE

There is rarely if ever an excuse for going over the presentation time you've been allotted. Listen to EMINEM, "Don't LOSE YOURSELF in the moment." It doesn't matter why. Get rid of these excuses:

- It doesn't matter if you started late.

- It doesn't matter if you have more content to share.

- It doesn't matter if someone (or something) hijacked your presentation.

In the corporate world, there's no Academy Awards music to play you off the stage. You can always finish early, but you should never go over. Of course, that means you, the presenter, need to know the time. Here are five hacks to alert you to time and adhere to the Cardinal Rule of timing:

1. There is an app for that. Get a timer for your phone, watch, or tablet.

2. Go analog. Have someone at the back of the room with three signs: 5 (minutes), 2 (minutes), and a big fat zero (STOP!).

3. Click it. Buy a clicker that has a timer built-in.

4. Use presenter mode on your laptop. It has a clock.

5. Take Q & A before you finish your presentation. If you know you have five minutes for a final story, wrap-up, and your call to action, then take questions at 10 minutes from finishing. At six minutes, answer the last question and go directly into your close. Or if you are presenting and get to Q & A with five minutes left, politely skip the Q & A, and go to your close. It's

a good practice to alert your room monitor or meeting host on how you plan to close, or they might hijack your presentation after Q & A or after you're finished the presentation with "Does anyone have any questions for Stan?"

"I learned this bonus tip from Milo Shapiro: Before every presentation, I ask clients what I should do if my presentation starts late: go the full time (ex: 60 minutes) or cut my content and end on schedule. This is a big issue as events are frequently running behind. Getting clarity from the client ahead of time helps.

Two examples:
1. One client said, "End on time." The event was running 20 minutes late, so I had to cut 20 minutes of content from a 60 minute presentation on the fly. Fortunately, I design my presentations with flexibility in mind and I made it happen.
2. Another client said, "Go the full 60 minutes," even though we were nearly 30 minutes behind. However, I sensed audience members would be nervous about the clock, so I started my presentation by sharing the agenda update and assuring them they wouldn't miss anything."

— Jeff Toister

"A lot of meeting and class rooms don't have clocks in them anymore! It's getting to be like Vegas out here! That's why I use Presentation Timer. It's an app on my phone, and I can prop it up on my computer to let me know where

Continued . . .

I am in the presentation, time-wise. It not only gives me presentation timing, it gives me a visual display of a bar filling up. That way, I can see when I'm a quarter of the way through, half-way, 3/4, etc. Also, when I'm getting ready to close, the app changes color. When the colors change, I know I need to wrap up—because as you said, I don't want to go "into the red zone!"

— Laura Bergells

"I'm also a fan of setting a timer on my Apple Watch for 5 minutes before my time is up. When I get the silent tap on my wrist, it's time to wrap up."

— Evan Carroll

There is one loophole with regard to timing. Not all cultures see timeliness the same. It's a best practice to always confirm your ending time—"And my drop-dead time is 2:30, right?" Alan was in Eastern Europe last year for a presentation. As his presentation was about to start more than fifteen minutes late, Alan asked for confirmation on the ending time. His client sponsor seemed shocked, "No! Take as long as you need. We love what you've got and want more of it." Call this the Eastern exception. But in the Western world? Absolutely. End. On. Time. Don't look at your watch. It's a cue to the audience that time is moving, and moves them to look too. Use one of the hacks to keep time without raising your arm.

TIP #60 - No one is going to complain if your presentation ends 10 minutes early. No conference attendee will ask for a refund when you let them out and they're first in line at the snack table. Time is precious. Curate it carefully. Find a way to end on time. Always.

"As Keynote for most events I also have the chance to be Emcee on occasion. Can't tell you the way planners freak out over the com with the AV team as one presenter bleeds into another and ruins the whole meeting. No matter the content, no one cares. Be done on time or as close to it as possible."

— Jason Hewlett

PRACTICE

"We talkin' about practice." According to *Sports Illustrated* in 2002, "Allen Iverson gave us arguably the most famous press conference of all time, dropping the word 'practice' 22 times and giving the sports world a sound bite that would be repeated for decades to come."[49]

When it comes to presenting, there are many benefits to be gained from practicing. But first thing first, we talkin' about practice. There is a difference between practicing and rehearsing. Rehearsal is running through your content from start to finish. Practice is going through a small part to get it right.

Here's a simple observation: We rehearse too much, and practice too little. Why? Because we want to feel better, not get better.

TIP #61 - Practice the open and close twice as much as the middle. Think of practice along the lines of flying a plane. When are planes most likely to crash? Most accidents occur during take-offs and

---

49. https://www.si.com/nba/2017/05/05/
   allen-iverson-practice-rant-press-conference-anniversary-timeline

landings. Take the extra time to prepare, practice, and nail your openings/closings.

BUILD MUSCLE

Repetition builds muscle. We know this in reference to strength training, yet it applies to strengthen your other skills too. Practice until you master a skill. Then, and only then, should you move on to a new one.

No one is a natural. Presenting well is a skill that we need to hone.

TIP #62 - We must always be looking for opportunities to speak and flex our presentation muscles.

"Take advantage of every opportunity to practice your communication skills so that when important occasions arise, you will have the gift, the style, the sharpness, the clarity, and the emotions to affect other people."

— Jim Rohn

TALKING ABOUT TIME

The end of your presentation is the only time people care about. Don't say you're short, running out, surprised by the time, watching the time, or even aware of the time. But ALWAYS end on time!

TIP #63 - Stop talking about time. Ever.

LENGTH

How long should your presentation be? Let's look for inspiration from three late Presidents:

From Franklin Delano Roosevelt, "Be sincere. Be brief. Be seated."

On November 19, 1863, the town of Gettysburg, Pennsylvania held a memorial to provide closure and dedicate the cemetery where thousands of men who died in the horrific battle the previous summer were buried. It doubled as a propaganda event to stoke the fires of the war effort. As the town leaders planned the event, they recognized they needed a speaker. They asked . . .

Edward Everett. Former Governor and Secretary of Education. A lifelong politician and known orator. He accepted with little fanfare. And then the event grew. And grew. It became a big deal. So the leaders reached out to the sitting president, Abraham Lincoln. To their surprise, he accepted, just 30 days before the scheduled event. But oops! They'd already given away the keynote. So Mr. Lincoln was asked to close out the event.

Edward Everett's speech that day was 13,607 words. Given that the average person speaks at somewhere between 125 and 150 words per minute, historians have estimated it took about two hours to deliver. Outside. In November. In Pennsylvania. With limited seating and a "Comfort Station" (tent) several hundred yards away. When Everett was finished speaking, President Lincoln gave the benediction. In only 272 words, we have a great speech that school children have memorized for over 150 years. Edward Everett wrote the President the next day, "I should be glad if I could flatter myself that I came as near to the central idea of the occasion, in two hours, as you did in two minutes."

A great lesson from President #16. Another from President #9. William Henry Harrison was excited to show the American public that he was not only a war hero but an educated man and capable leader. On March 4, 1841, he delivered his inaugural address. All 8,455 words of it. In a near-freezing rain. Without a coat. And he caught pneumonia. And died 31 days later. He was (is) the shortest-term president in American history.

The moral? Long talks kill people. Don't do it.

TIP #64 - Your presentation should be as short as needed to accomplish your objectives and share your central idea.

We've finished the 10 keys to being Loud and Clear. Now, let's examine the S.I.L.V.E.R. framework for planning and delivering your presentation.

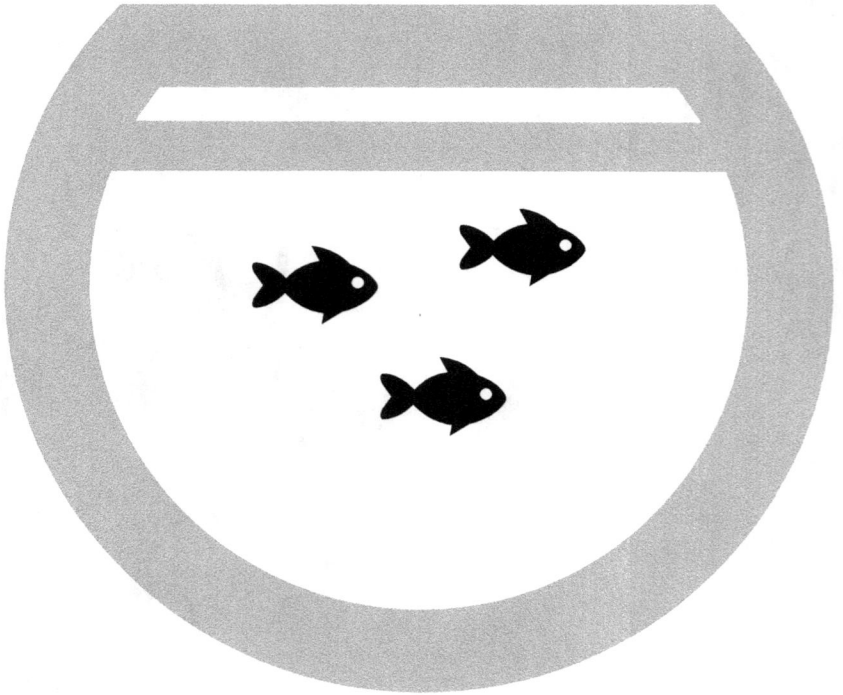

PRESENTATION PLANNING (THE HOW)

CHAPTER 16

STARTING

"Begin with the end in mind."

— Stephen Covey

(Habit #2 of the *7 Habits of Highly Successful People*)

Can we go ahead and agree that if your presentation, pitch, or update is longer than one sentence, your audience is likely to—no, they *will*—forget some of your content? Does that make presenting seem futile? Perhaps.

But the goal of a presenter is not for an audience to repeat everything you say. After all, it likely took you years to obtain the knowledge you're trying to share with them. They're not going to know what you know after 50 minutes or a full day. You want them to walk away and repeat the core message of the presentation. ("This is the most important thing to remember . . . ") After that, it's getting them to *want* more. The information is available. You have it! They have to want it.

We think the best way to get an audience to follow along and be able to connect their own experience and questions to your content is to have a structure that is simple, memorable, and repeatable. And along the way you'll want to be entertaining. Good visuals are important. But none of that is likely to come together if you don't have a plan. You need a strategy for meeting your objectives. You need to know how to get started.

Most of the clients Alan coaches want to start with PowerPoint. And it's an important part of the presentation. Get it right. But it's not the first thing you should do.

Many experts will immediately want to give details and correct any misconceptions. There will be lots of detail and explanations. That's important, but it's not the first thing you should do.

Experienced presenters may recognize the importance of opening and ending well and the power of a story. That's a key, but it's not the first thing you should do.

Before you begin to craft your message, your structure, your metaphor, or your slides, answer two very important questions:

> Who am I presenting to?

> Why am I presenting?

The answers to those questions will lead you to the promised land. The land where audiences sing your praises, buy your products, and tell everyone else about you. But miss those questions and you're just spewing information. And no matter how good your information, it's just information.

KNOW YOUR AUDIENCE

While the temptation to start writing or start creating slides or start storytelling is great, stop. Spend some time in thought. Think about the people in the seats listening to you. Here are 11 questions to get you started:

1. Why are they there?
2. What pains are they experiencing?
3. What is it that they want to hear?
4. What do you think they need to hear?
5. What knowledge level or experience do they have with your topic?
6. What will they want or need to do next?
7. What disconnect might there be between your culture, demographic, or philosophy and theirs?
8. How do they feel about you?
9. What is their overall goal?
10. What is their goal for their time with you?
11. How will they make decisions if you're asking them to do something?

Consider some basic answers to those questions and how that would guide your presentation:

- If the major reason the audience is there is to get continuing ed credit, then they want some content. But often they just want it to be over. Amp up the lighthearted anecdotes and the stories. Case studies and examples are key. Shine with your experience. Drop the theory—they know it already.

- If you're 20 years older than the majority of the audience (or 40), then drop the references to material things, raising children, and the Challenger disaster.

- If the audience is the executive team, consider further if they're big picture folks (CEO probably is) or detail folks (CTO probably is). They'll want to engage you. Prepare for questions. Lead with the results.

- If the audience is highly motivated for success but hasn't had it (for example, average presenters listening to a presentation on presentation skills), then ask why not. Is it a knowledge problem (rare)? Motivation problem? (But you said they were motivated.) Habit problem? (Bingo!)

- If they're beginners (and you're not), ask yourself how they would best learn what you know, and how much they need to know today. Rome wasn't built in a day. Perhaps today you survey the land. Lay the foundation for the Coliseum tomorrow.

Most audiences want results. They want shorter sales cycles, less overhead, more efficient workers, fewer headaches, more customers, simpler technology, easier access. You get the idea.

But wanting results doesn't always produce results. What they *need* is a roadmap or guide on how to get there. For instance, people want painless, quick, foolproof methods to present better (a silver bullet). And they want to feel better. But what they need are techniques and practice that lead to skills. Skills that give them good experiences that build their confidence. It's not short. Ever. We must address what it takes.

Better than thinking about your audience, get on the phone with them. Find someone who represents the audience and ask them. They'll be glad to help.

KNOW YOUR ROLE

Once we know what the audience needs (and wants), we must assess our role in getting them there. Remember, we're the conduit between them and the information they need. Whether you call yourself a coach or not, we absolutely love this concept and definition. The word coach comes from the seventeenth century. It is a shortened version of stagecoach, a covered carriage that takes people of importance from where they are to where they want or need to be.[50]

First, we protect our audience. Cover them. Don't let them get confused. Or bored.

Next, we treat them as though they are important. No reason to talk down to them or make fun of where they are (or aren't).

Finally, we get them to where they need to be. It may not be where they want to be, but it's where they need to be. They may need to curtail expenses. They may need to change the settings in their .ini file on the server. They may need to rewrite some marketing copy. They may need to change their system of contacting prospects. They may need to spend some money (with you!) to get a service they could never produce on their own. You're the expert. You're the guide. Lead them to where they need to be.

Ultimately, in the business world you're probably helping your audience solve a problem, sell a product, or make a decision. It involves information. But it also involves moving people emotionally to a place

---

50. https://keithwebb.com/why-the-origin-of-the-word-coach-matters/

where they would be ready to make a decision. You can't make them decide, buy, or act. But you can make an option very enticing and attractive. Presenting sounds a little like sales. And that's because it is.

CREATE A SYSTEM

Even if you have all the facts and nuggets your audience needs and wants, you still have to transfer the material to them in such a way that they can use it when they need it most. It's no different than learning math, or cooking, or sales methodology. Anyone can follow along with the instructor. But teachers don't know if they are successful until their students take the test.

The best system is the one that works. And that could be different for different people. But without knowing intimate details about the brain patterns of your audience (you probably don't know that about your own family, much less your team or client), you do what works the best most often. And that's giving your roadmap a structure.

Consider this example, stolen unashamedly from Harold Stolovitch's material. Without looking, which direction do the presidents on the penny, nickel, dime, and quarter face?

Would you bet the money on it?

Now go look at some change (or Google it).

- Penny - Abe looks right

- Nickel - Thomas looks left

- Dime - Teddy looks left

- Quarter - George looks left

If I ask you in a month, could you get it? I could lecture all day and you'd still probably forget. But if I say, "Abe Lincoln did RIGHT by the people; he LEFT all the other presidents behind," you'll have the answer and a mechanism/structure to recall it the rest of your life.

That's the sort of task that faces us as presenters. How can we get what we know into the minds of our audience for the long haul? It's not by adding more bullets to the slide, we know that. But there's got to be some sort of structure or mnemonic or device. Even a story. Somehow, some way, find a method to make your facts make sense.

Notice that we've not mentioned the order of our presentation. That's because the human brain doesn't function that way. We read in a linear fashion (page 10 before page 100). But we think interconnectedly. Find the categories that connect your points. Focus on the categories. Don't add detail until you have that solid. That's probably all the level of detail your audience will remember anyway.

But if we've understood where our important people need to go and have a roadmap with some easy-to-remember categories, then all we have to do is add detail until our time is up. Let's talk about illustrating our points.

CHAPTER 17

ILLUSTRATING

*"The illustration is merely a vehicle to convey
a point of view."*

— Michael Ramirez

S adly, many presenters in the business world think that the only way to present information is through PowerPoint. Alan asked a guy one time to give him some thoughts on mentoring. The man was a little older than Alan and had run a mentoring program for decades. When the two of them sat down together at Panera Bread, the mentor opened his laptop and scrolled through about 50 slides. With just one person in the audience! Alan said what he wanted (and needed) was some ideas. A fresh look on things. Some great stories to get him going.

One of the things Alan does in his presentation skills classes is teach for two days without ever turning on a computer. Not because he doesn't know how to use one but because some people have never seen that done before. Colleges use PowerPoint as the de facto lecturing tool. Kindergarten classes are requiring kids to present from it. We've adopted the word "presentation" to mean the deck of slides itself. This has become a common question: "Would you send me the presentation before the meeting?"

But PowerPoint is NOT the only way (and frequently not the best way) to present material. It may be the most used way. It may be the easiest (for you) way. It may be the most accepted way. But as you set about to present, ask yourself what is the best way to present this material?

We're intersecting with what trainers and teachers call instructional design. The canonical accepted method is ADDIE:

- Analysis
- Design
- Development
- Implementation
- Evaluation

You could take weeks of training or even get a PhD. in this field. But at the core all you need to do is match what your audience wants and needs with what you are able to provide.

The goal is to come up with a plan for how the audience will "get" the information. You may not see yourself as a teacher. You were asked to present the quarterly numbers or discuss the optimization parameters of the web server. No matter. You are teaching. Remember the audience's needs and wants. They need a roadmap to get the results they want.

What method you use to present is dependent on several parameters:

- How many people are in the audience?
- What is their existing knowledge level?
- How much room (space) do you have?
- How much time do you have?
- What is your skill level in facilitation? Presenting? Answering questions?
- What is the audience's culture of participation?
- What time of day is it?

You can start with one basic question: Does your audience (or at least most of them) already know the material? If the answer is yes, then your job is not to present the material, your job is to extract the material from the minds of the audience. If they do not know what you're about to say, then your job is to make the material as interesting as possible so that it matters to them.

Once in his corporate job, Alan was forced to take an online training program to teach him how to evacuate the building in case of a fire or other emergency. In his words, "I'd be embarrassed if I had designed the program. It took over 30 minutes to complete, and I can sum it up in a sentence that you and everyone who's ever been in a building already know. Get out, as quickly and calmly as possible! Everyone already knew that."

METHODS OF PRESENTING

There are many options for how to present material and lead your audience to the conclusions they came to get. Lecturing (with or without PowerPoint) is probably the easiest, most efficient, and most accepted. But at least consider some others. Not all of these will work in all areas. But this is designed to get you thinking. Remember, differentiation is the key to success! If you're like everyone else, then you're forgotten much of the material by the end of the day. Here are four alternatives:

1. Exercises / Activities - You didn't learn algebra from listening. You had to do the problems. If you're trying to get someone to operate a device or software, exercises might be a better way.

2. Video - If it's just a talking head, a live talking head is better. But if there are moving parts or an emotional lesson, consider a short (keyword: short) video.

3. Games - Alan remembers an example from an instructional design course he took discussing games. The particular challenge from this consultant was a (required) two-day workshop going over some government regulations for a group of about 100. The previous year, the trainer had read slides going over the regulations. "And next we turn to part 3, section B, subheading iii . . . " The mic volume better have been loud because of all the snoring.

   This trainer, a worldwide leader in using games in corporate settings, spent some of his well-earned fee on door prizes. The grand prize was two round-trip airline tickets! He divided the group into teams. He passed out the hefty regulations. Then he described the game show they would play on the second day (something akin to Family Feud or Wheel of Fortune). Each group was to come up with questions from the material and the emcee would use their questions as the game show puzzlers. Then he walked off the stage and didn't do ANYTHING until the end of Day One. He and his team collected the questions and prepared the game show for the following day. So what happened?

The groups split off and were pouring through the regulations, trying to come up with real puzzlers to stump the other groups. One man tried to take a break from his group and one of his team members chastised him. "We're going to win this thing. You get over here and help us right now!"

The second day, there was so much energy in the room. The groups arrived early and stayed for every last minute. What a great way to make boring content exciting!

Alan has seen Lego blocks used as prizes for week-long sales training and people would nearly fight to participate to get a coveted block.

4. Panels - When working with Athletic Directors about changing culture in sports, we put a principal, head football coach, and booster club president on stage and ran a panel discussion with a moderator (to keep things on track and moving). The audience was riveted. We could have lectured on the same material, but hearing from the people in the trenches, live, was better than any presenter could do.

Our opening warning bears repeating. Every technique may not work in every setting. Software developers are a very different crowd from sales account managers. Know what works before you step on stage. But do consider that PowerPoint and your voice may not be the answer.

Notes, quotes, jokes (danger!), questions, debrief, group discussions, polls, quizzes, interview, giving job assignments/role playing, movement (seating?), fishbowl. All of these methods might be better than just you and your slides.

Need ideas or not sure how to implement any of these? Google (or a phone call to an instructional designer friend) may help.

Next, we turn our attention to developing your skills.

CHAPTER 18

LEARNING

"I warm up at home. I hit the stage, I'm ready."

— Louis Armstrong

Height ow did you learn to ride a bicycle? Throw a baseball? Bake cookies? Use your computer? Manage a meeting? Tell a story?

Our experience in education and life tells us it's probably some combination of three things:

- Personal study

- The direction of a teacher or mentor

- Past experience and imitation

We like to think in the Information Age that we can learn anything. Ask YouTube how to tell a story and you'll have several dozen options, ranging from internationally renowned speech coaches to TED talks to people you've never heard of who know how to optimize social media. My guess is you'll only watch a few. What will you learn? More importantly, what will you apply? Probably very little. You'll tell your next story in similar way as you told your last one. That's because storytelling and presenting in general are not academic exercises you can pass with a #2 pencil and a bubble sheet. You need to learn it.

Of more importance to most of us is the influence and instruction of someone we trust. A mentor. A true mentor who is interested in you becoming better won't just teach you. He or she will make you practice, check on you, and hold your feet to the fire until you get it right. We only tolerate this sort of intimacy and accountability from people we trust. A respected leader. Perhaps that person intersects with your YouTube search. Perhaps you read a book by two guys who have spent the last few decades speaking and decided to share what they learned in a book named after a fish and a color. If you trust someone, you're a whole lot more likely to follow their advice. We're grateful you've read this far, but now it's time to apply what we're talking about.

When it comes to presenting (or any habit-based endeavor), the teacher you listen to most is probably the one of experience and imitation. If you walk into any organization and watch five presentations, you've likely seen them all. If you're new to the corporate world, then you watch and listen. When it's your turn on stage, you do what others do. Your slides look like everyone else's. Your position in the room is modeled after everyone else's. Your tone and demeanor, dress and attitude, open and close, content and structure—it's the same. Oh sure, there are rebels and outliers, but people don't mimic them. They're a sideshow. The effect of culture is to create people who behave similarly.

The problem in the presentation world is that much of the behavior we take on and mimic is not good. We spend precious little time actively learning and applying and mostly "pick things up." Alan has noticed this in the sarcasm level of his two children. "Where'd they get that?" Alan says as he points at himself. "We've never had a lesson on sarcasm in our household, and yet my children are experts." This mimicry is even more prevalent in the presentation universe. It appears we're all giving quite similar presentations.

Except for those who aren't. And they all have one amazingly common attribute. They've made a conscious effort to be different. They've become good not only at presenting but also at learning about presenting.

When Alan was starting out on his presentation journey, he jumped at the opportunity to hear a talk. Any talk. He'd take notes on what the speaker did. He'd observe the good, the bad, and the ugly. He'd watch for the audience's reaction. He'd try to categorize what was a skill and what was the personality of the speaker. He found out two important things:

- Almost everything that he liked could be replicated. (This was skill, not talent.)

- No one was self-taught.

When he asked how they got good at their speaking, he always got the same answer: a time, a place, and a person. They had someone teach them, and they worked at it.

> "I schedule time in my calendar to prepare a few days prior to a presentation not long after booking the event. I have a system I follow that helps me be fully prepared for the day of the engagement."
>
> — Dave Crenshaw

Zig Ziglar practiced two hours every night in his hotel before speaking—after 30 years of experience! Most of the TEDx speakers we've been around have spent upwards of 100 hours (or more) for their 18 minutes on the red dot. This must take work!

Sadly, most people get up to speak with the same goal. To get through it. But every time you present is a chance to get better. As the adage in sports goes, "Champions are made in the offseason."

Hitting a baseball from a professional pitcher is described as the hardest skill in sports. You can make the Hall of Fame if you're successful a third of the time. Fully one-fifth of major leaguers strike out (the worst outcome for a hitter). Hitters don't get better while they are facing the pitcher. Hitters get better in the cage, at practice taking soft-toss, or in the clubhouse studying their swing on video. Albert Puhols has had his swing described as the "smoothest in the game." But even now, a presumptive Hall of Famer, he takes a thousand swings a day. He wasn't BORN with a great swing; he developed it.

And you (and everybody else) weren't born speaking well. You weren't born speaking at all! If you want to be great, you're going to have to work at it.

Ben Franklin was a master student of just about everything. One of the great orators of his day was the evangelist George Whitfield. Ben described him this way: "By hearing him often I came to distinguish easily between sermons newly composed and those which he had often preached in the course of this travels. His delivery of the latter was so improved by frequent repetitions that every accent, every emphasis, every modulation of voice was so perfectly well turned and well placed that, without being interested in the subject, one could not help being pleased with the discourse, a pleasure of much the same kind with that received from an excellent piece of music." Those sorts of responses don't come to someone only willing to do a single performance with no practice.

Reading a book about presentations is a great first step, but you're going to have to do more than that. Learning is only useful if it's applied. Here are three ways to revitalize your presentation self and become a fundamentally better speaker.

1. Fall in love with Mr. Canon

2. Find someone to help you on your journey

3. Try something different

FALL IN LOVE WITH MR. CANON

So much of presenting is in the head of the presenter. Remember, we act according to what we believe is true (whether it's true or not). If you think you're speaking loud enough, then you're not likely to increase your volume. If you believe your movement is acceptable, you'll not work actively to change it. If putting your arms far from your body feels weird, you'll not likely express very big.

But those views of yourself change when you see what's REALLY happening. And no coach or audience member is likely to convince you of that. So we hire a certified expert in the field of telling the Truth. Our assistant is called Mr. Canon. (He has friends: Mr. Nikon, Mr. Sony, Mr. iPhone, Mr. Samsung.) The reason we can trust him is that he tells the truth. He shows that your hands never stop moving. He shows that you were never more than arms-length from your laptop. He shows that you didn't smile when you said you were happy to be here. He shows that your eyes were on your slides more than your audience.

No one seems to like Mr. Canon. It must be lonely to be him. But for those who listen to his advice, they crave his input. It's the only way we can truly convince ourselves of what needs to change.

Mr. Canon needn't be an unwelcome or distracting visitor in the room. You can use your phone, leaned against a drink glass at the banquet. You can ask for a recording from the host or use the built-in function of a web host. You can use your computer to record your phone conversations for further review.

The most important aspect of Mr. Canon is that you listen/watch him. A pastor once mentioned that his church videotaped all his messages. For thirty years. When pressed further, he admitted that he had never watched a single one of them. He was likely delivering in the same style he did 30 years ago.

Great athletes video and watch every single play that they're involved in. Even in practice. Great speakers do the same thing. Be like the great speakers and evaluate yourself rigorously. Define and describe exactly what needs to change.

Mr. Canon is the first stop on your journey to change your presenting behavior. But he shouldn't be the only stop.

FIND SOMEONE TO HELP YOU ON YOUR JOURNEY

Even if we recognize what is broken, we usually are helpless to change our behavior. Dr. Barry Borgerson came through our two-day skills workshop. Barry is the author of *The Auto-Self: The Key to Creating Star Performers and Becoming a Star Yourself* and is an expert in changing human behavior. When asked what we could do to help speakers change their habits, his answer was direct and clear: "Stop the behaviors that need changing as soon as they happen. Be clear about what needs changing. And have them immediately try again."

It turns out this is the same thing we need to do to lose weight, be kinder to our family, and change our tendency to tailgate. Identify the bad behavior at the moment it happens. Outline the correction. Try again.

Even if we fall in love with Mr. Canon, we are powerless to change ourselves through merely identifying what needs fixing. We need the kind correction of someone else. It could be a coach, trusted mentor, boss, or family member.

Friend and colleague Kevin Snyder has been a successful keynote presenter for over a decade. He's spoken in every US state to over a thousand audiences. But when he has a new talk coming up or is chasing the World Champion of Public Speaking title from Toastmasters, he enlists others to change his behavior.

Who can you find who will give you good direction on changing your behavior?

TRY SOMETHING DIFFERENT

The last piece of behavior change is by far the toughest. Actually changing our behavior.

When middle age and its metabolism slowdown hit, I (Alan) experienced the expected weight gain. I went to a nutritionist for help. (Mr. Canon had already identified the problem: a spare tire.) I opened the conversation with an honest appraisal of the situation. "Ms. Nutritionist, you need to understand one thing about me. I love to eat." It was true and almost a 12-steps admission. "Hi, I'm Alan, and I love to eat." Her response was quick, direct, and identified not only the problem but the way forward. "Are you willing to change what you eat and how much you eat?" She then educated me on the choices I had to make. She gave me principles that I could follow. She told me that my body doesn't tell me what it needs for me to eat. It only tells me when it's hungry. She gave me visual helpers to assist with my decisions in the moment of truth (one of the lasting impressions was the volume difference in 100 calories of grapes and 100 calories of raisins. Same food, mostly the same nutrients, but an eight-fold difference in volume. Grapes would fill me up eight times faster than raisins for the same caloric intake!) I proceeded to lose almost 20 pounds (which I regained when I began traveling a lot, and then lost through stress, then gained through indifference, then lost . . . sigh. Pass the ice cream.) Most people with weight problems (myself included) simply aren't willing or able to change their behavior on their own. (Side note: both in saving money and losing weight, most experts agree that cataloging your entire intake is a great step in changing behavior.)

If we apply the principles from behavior change to presentation skills, we need principles that will guide our decision. We need to know what decisions to make in the moments on stage. And we'll need some accountability, either through a log, video, or personal coach to enact the changes.

Most presenters are comfortable with the results they get. Which isn't saying much. The biggest competitor to a speech coach is apathy.

Here are some questions to consider. Are you willing to:

- change how you present?
- raise your voice?
- shorten your details?
- tell that story in two minutes instead of five?
- let your audience ask questions whenever they want?
- present without slides?
- turn the lights on?
- use a different clicker?
- dress differently?
- write your entire presentation before you ever make a slide in PowerPoint?

If your first response is, "Well, ... but... no...", then you aren't likely to change. So expect the same results.

THE FORMULA FOR CHANGE

There is an interesting model about changing culture. Alan was exposed to it through his experience coaching sports. It's called the Formula for Change, created by David Gleicher in the early 1960s and refined by Kathie Dannemiller in the 1980s. It applies to so many things we want to change in life, including presenting. The formula is:

$$C = D \times V \times FS > R$$

Here's how it breaks down:

> Change (C = something done differently) only happens when the product created by your discontent (D = you don't like the way things are) multiplied by your vision (V = your clarity in what could be) combined with your first steps (FS = the action you take) is greater than the resistance (R) in not overcoming the problem.

If your primary resistance lies in the fact that you don't have (or don't make) the time to practice, no amount of vision or discontent will make you a better presenter. If you have no vision for what could be (you don't know what to do), your product is zero, and you cannot overcome any resistance. But if you have enough discontent (I'm tired of boring people in my presentations, I mean *really* tired!), enough vision (I've read *Silver Goldfish* and know exactly what to do!), and enough first steps and practice (I'm going to a workshop, going to videotape myself, and hire a coach to help me get great!), then anyone can become a great presenter. That's our core belief. Anyone can do this.

But experience shows not everyone will. The Formula for Change tells us why.

PUTTING IN THE PRACTICE

How much people practice is very telling about their attitude about presenting. Speaking Coach Stephanie Scotti estimates TEDx speakers seem to average about 80-100 hours for an 18 minute (or less) presentation. Sounds important.

Group managers probably prepare less than ten minutes for their weekly hour-long meeting. Doesn't sound important.

Head football coaches in the NFL put in 100 hours of preparation for a three-hour game. Sounds important.

Recreational coaches ask the players what they want to do at practice. Doesn't sound important.

We frequently hear, "But I don't have time to practice." People find time to do what's important to them. And if the presentation matters, you'll find time to practice.

But there are two types of practice: practicing your skill and practicing your talk.

Once you have a skill, you can focus on execution and strategy. Without the skill, no amount of strategy will help. The authors of this book easily have over 20,000 hours of speaking on stage. That's a lot of hours. Not all of them were good hours. But we're good enough by now that we don't need to practice walking up on stage, wiring our microphone, or changing our tone of voice. But we absolutely need to practice our opening lines, our call to action, asking the right questions, and the effective use of a pause at the right time. Stan doesn't need to practice his rooftop bar in NYC story—he's got a 30-second and three-minute version ready to go at any time. Alan can tell you the Gettysburg address story in his sleep. But when we have new material or are preparing a client proposal, we have to practice to be good.

Only you and Mr. Canon know how your skill level compares to what you want it to be. If you haven't received the honest feedback you need to know where you stand, you'd be wise to find it. You can practice your skills all day, every day. Family dinner, elevator conversations, ordering your meal from your waiter, talking to a cashier, phone conversations, updates with your boss—every time you open your mouth you can get better. If you view speaking skills as something "always on," then you are always ready. If you are trying to master "presentation skills," you have limited chance to practice.

But practicing/rehearsing your particular presentation is not something you are likely do at the family dinner table. What should you practice if you can't get blocks of time to do your whole presentation? Here are the pieces that need the most work:

- Your open and close
- Segues between your structure/categories
- Your ask
- Your story setups and conclusions
- The pauses between any sentences
- The numbers that matter
- Your interaction with your slides

If you get those right, the stuff in between will be fine. We're not saying never to practice the rest, but it'll work out OK.

We know you are busy. You don't have spare time. How can you steal practice time? Here are four places you can practice your presentation:

- In the car - connect your phone to Bluetooth. Hit record on your voice recorder app. Speak and then play it back. Practice stories between stoplights. Get a feel for how long a minute is on the highway and find a way to close.
- In the shower
- Walking the dog

- Though we made fun of it, why not family dinner—you'll likely get some great feedback.

Bored of practice? Been at it too long? Here are some innovative ways to keep practice fresh.

- Give your presentation backwards. Start at the end and end at the start.

- Mix up some flashcards of your major sections. Draw a card and start there.

- Work through your "one-sentence" version. Each point only gets one sentence.

- Set the timer. Pick some random time and try to guess where you'll be when the timer goes off.

Three aspects of practice that make it more valuable:

- Practice out loud. Working through text in your mind is not the same as saying it out loud. You'll find words and phrases that may not work for you when you say them.

- Practice with gestures. Actors use this to help them remember their lines. The lines and the gestures go hand-in-hand. You don't get one without the other.

- Practice at the same time of day as your presentation. Your body will be in a similar energy state and you'll be ready.

PRACTICE WITH SLIDES

PowerPoint is a tool. Tool usage can always be better. It's true of hand saws, staple guns, hammers, and PowerPoint. One of the sure signs that presenters are not well-versed in the use of the tool and their own slides in particular is when they turn their heads on every slide or are constantly looking at the screen. If you know your tool and know your content, you only need a glance, which could be to a confidence monitor, the originating laptop, or a mirroring tool to confirm the tool is doing its job, and you can get back to the much more important task of delivering content to your audience. There are several features of PowerPoint that are worth knowing about and practicing. They'll make your visual presentation smooth and professional-looking. But did we mention it takes practice?

A GOOD REMOTE

Assuming the space and the culture will allow it, moving about the stage and room is a great way to look confident and engage your audience. But if you're driving slides, you'll need a remote control for your computer. Most remotes have a little USB transmitter that you plug in to the computer so you can carry the remote around with you. They range in size and functionality. Most are RF, not infrared, which means they do not need to be pointed at the computer. Just click the button to advance. Alan uses a "ring" remote, which fits (barely) on his pinky finger and allows him to gesture without slinging a remote across the room. Stan uses a Cue remote. Whatever remote you use, practice with it until you're comfortable with its operation.

THE B KEY

One of the best kept secrets of PowerPoint is the B key. When in slideshow mode, this blanks the screen into a solid black screen. W does the same thing, except the blank screen is white. Hit any key and the show resumes on the previous slide. Most remotes built in the last decade also have a blank button, so you can do this remotely as well. If you find yourself talking about something other than what is displaying, just blank out the screen and resume when the visual matches your subject again.

HIDE SLIDES OR JUMP TO SLIDES

Most people think, and use, PowerPoint linearly. That is, in order. Slide one comes first, then slide two, until "End of slide show, click to exit." shows up. Most people know you can hide slides. That way they don't show up in a show. But you can also jump to any slide in your show, including hidden slides, with the jump to feature. Just type in the number of your slide and hit <Enter>. Type in 3-2-Enter and you'll go to slide 32, even if it's hidden. That way you can skip whole sections of slides if you're running behind or you find out they don't apply to your audience. You can also prepare "just in case" slides, and then jump to them if your audience has a question that the visual addresses. You only need the slide number. Print out an index to leave next to your computer so you can easily find out what slide applies. This is much more professional than scrolling through fifty slides and their animations to get to another part of your presentation.

PRESENTER VIEW

A real asset when using PowerPoint is Presenter View. As its name implies, this is a view only the Presenter sees. Setting up Presenter View requires a few steps before you start your show, so come a few minutes early. You have to set up a second display (what the audience sees) and toggle PowerPoint to use it. Once it's in place, there are several advantages for the presenter.

- You have a clock.
- You can create a visual index of all your slides (including hidden ones) and also an index of sections and jump to any one of them with a click.
- You can see the next slide or at least what happens when you click next.
- You can see your presenter notes.

Again, the audience sees none of this. They see only the slide you are displaying.

EXAMPLE: PRESENTER VIEW

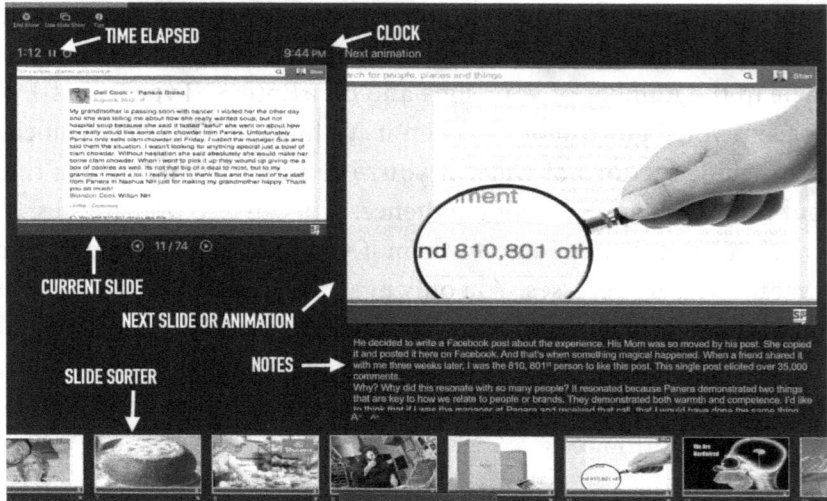

TIME ELAPSED

CLOCK

1:12

9:44 PM Next animation

11 / 74

CURRENT SLIDE

NEXT SLIDE OR ANIMATION

SLIDE SORTER

NOTES

CONFIDENCE MONITORS AND MIRRORING

At some conferences, a confidence monitor is provided at the feet of the presenter or perhaps in the back of the room. These are usually mirroring what the audience sees. That's nice, but it's better to mirror what's on your screen, especially if it's in Presenter View. There are other solutions to mirroring a screen. One we've found that works with both PC and Mac (although the client only works on iPad) is Doceri.[51] It requires a WiFi network with peer-to-peer connectivity, which is not always possible in a public conference or client guest network. If that's the case, it won't work. Once set up, it will display whatever is on your laptop or your iPad, which can be anywhere. This allows the presenter to see their control screen. It might not be necessary, but it even allows you to control the remote computer by touch (for instance to advance the slides). Doceri is $30, and does take some setup time to get working.

---

51. https://doceri.com

PREPARING FOR GAME DAY

Here are three tips for preparing on the day (or eve) of your presentation:

- Get as much good sleep as you can. Staying up all night is not advised.

- Don't use drugs or alcohol to relax.

- Hydrate the day before. Drinking before you get on stage only increases the pressure, if you know what we mean.

Now we turn our attention to starting your presentation.

CHAPTER 19

VAULTING

"I've learned that people will forget what you said, people will forget what you did, but people will never forget how you made them feel."

— Maya Angelou

Alan's first coaching client was a friend. Super smart. A rising star in his field. He'd been invited to speak at a large conference. It was understood that this was an audition for the national stage, tremendous exposure, and a huge professional feather in his cap. It was important to him.

He invited Alan to come to a dry run of his talk at a lunch-and-learn. When it was over, they debriefed. Alan asked his friend how he thought he did. He answered, "I don't know. I didn't think it was great. I felt like I lost their attention somewhere." Their friendship allowed for some degree of sarcasm. Alan shook his head and politely disagreed. "You didn't lose your audience's attention. You never had it." His friend had executed on a worn old theme with what's called the "TCP," the Typical Corporate Presentation. It's no wonder he defaulted to that. It's done a zillion times a day all over the world.

Speaker comment in the TCP	Sarcastic audience response
Hi, My name is ___	Wow! That matches what's on the title slide and the schedule!
I'm so glad to be here today.	Then why aren't you smiling?
I'm here to talk about ___	Again, that matches what's in the program! Wow!
Thanks to ___ for inviting me.	I wonder how much he's getting paid?
Before we get started . . .	It's too late for that.
You need to know a little about me . . .	I already stalked you on social media and know more than you want me to know.
Now let's find out about you. How many of you ___?	I didn't come to listen to these people talk.

Let's go over our agenda.	Let's talk about something important.
Note that I have far too much information for this tiny time slot, so please listen fast.	Did they not tell you how long your own talk was?
Some housekeeping rules. I'll take questions at the end.	Except you'll have run over, and we'll all want to leave by then.
Let's make sure you know that I won't cover . . .	Can we stop wasting time and cover what you said you would cover?
Here are some basic definitions to make sure we're all on the same page	Why? Did the dumb people not read the description ahead of time?
And now let's dive right in . . .	Feels like a belly flop to me.

ZZZZzzzzzzzzzz.

YOU CAN'T LOSE WHAT YOU DON'T HAVE

Your audience's attention must be earned, starting with the very first words out of your mouth.

How you open is a critical component of any speaking engagement. *Forbes* says that you make a first impression in seven seconds. By the time you finish your first paragraph, they've already formed an opinion of you. If you're, well, *typical*, then the opinion isn't likely to be extraordinary. The goal is to make a positive splash and have them ready to listen and excited to hear what you have to say.

If we only have seven seconds, then the pleasantries and throwaway phrases have got to go. No "I'm happy to be here in Dallas today." Drop the parade of "Thank you so much for . . ." Quit telling them what you're going to talk about. They either already know or they don't care. And for Pete's sake (and everyone else's), don't open with a joke you copied from the Internet. Just get to it.

But what is "it"? What is the opening that works for the presenter and audience alike?

As we saw in chapter 7, the ability to Connect is what makes an audience want to listen. Stories transcend age, culture, and demographic to connect better than any other technique.

The opening of the story is critical. Think about your favorite book or movie. They NEVER open with "This is a story about . . . " or "Let me tell you a story." They introduce the setting and get to the conflict before the first chapter is over or the opening credits roll. "A long time ago, in a galaxy far, far away . . . " (*Star Wars*) "It was the best of times, it was the worst of times . . . " (*A Tale of Two Cities*) "It was a bright cold day in April, and the clocks were striking thirteen." (*1984*) "You better not never tell nobody but God." (*The Color Purple*—what a great title!) From the visual of the ball chasing Indiana Jones in *Raiders of the Lost Ark* or the simple uttering of "Rosebud" in *Citizen Kane*, the audience's interest is piqued. You have far too much at stake to ramble on. Get to it! Quickly!

Don't tell a story for story sake. The story needs to get the audience somewhere. And that somewhere is the main point you want to make. This is one of the most fun parts of crafting a presentation. Figure out what you want to say as you've done in chapter 11 "Simplify," chapter 12 "Objective," chapter 13 "Outline," and chapter 16 "Organization." Find the core message you want the audience to remember, and craft a story whose moral leads us to that destination.

While stories are far and away the best way to open in most circumstances, they certainly are not the only way that works. A dose of humor taken from the current group, crafting an analogy or a crafty use of metaphor, quoting an expert or using a reference, having a great picture or prop, introducing an acronym (like S.I.L.V.E.R.), using current events (which is likely just a story), or opening with a probing and thought-provoking question can all serve to grab your audience's attention and set you up for the message ahead.

Don't assume this only works in a presentation setting. Great openings set the tone for meetings, webinars, and interviews. Know what you're going to say from those very first words. Grab your audience's mind and get to the point!

CAPTURE THEIR ATTENTION

When Alan was a freshman in college, his major (engineering) made chemistry a required course. This was the chemistry class for non-chemistry folks. It was nicknamed "Chemistry for people who hate Chemistry." All it took was a C and you'd never see the periodic table again in your life.

The professor, of course, had a different view. He had—literally—written the text book on chemistry. He fairly bobbed into class, espousing the glories of chemistry and at one point exclaimed "Chemistry. Is. Life!"

On the first day of class, he announced a lab that he'd perform during our lecture. This was in a large lecture hall, three stories high, with maybe 350 students in the class. Ho hum. A yardstick. A candle taped to the end of it. A Bunsen burner. But wait, what's this?! The professor was climbing on top of the lab desk at the front of the lecture hall. All the while droning on about why we should care about chemistry. Standing on the lab desk, he reached up and grabbed a string, which we had failed to notice before. It was attached to a six-foot weather balloon suspended a couple of stories above our heads. He began to pull the balloon down. Closer. Closer. As it neared the mad professor in his lab coat, he reached down with the yardstick and lit the candle. About the time he muttered "hydrogen" and "heat," he lifted the candle to the balloon and . . .

BOOM!! This was not a little boom. This was full-on, fireball spewing, shockwave inducing, hear-it-across-campus BOOOOM. The class went berserk. Books flew. Girls (and boys) shrieked. The frat boys in the back fell into the aisle (which, given it was a Monday morning, may have happened anyway). It was mayhem for about a minute. The professor climbed down off the desk and simply said, "See, I told you chemistry was interesting."

He began multiple lectures that semester with, "Class, today you'll want to pay attention. We have a laboratory to show you." You bet! For a class I hated, it's astonishing that decades later I still remember some basic principles of chemistry, all because a professor knew how to get an audience's attention.

It's probably not recommended that you blow things up to get your audience's attention. Fire marshals tend to frown on such antics. But you have a wide world of ways to get your audience's attention, and none of them begin with, "I'm so happy to be here today" or "Hi, my name is Bob."

GIVE THEM A REASON TO LISTEN

One of the things Alan noticed when he started corporate training was that everyone entered workshops/classes with a low expectation. One evaluation comment got his attention and caused him to rethink how he approached training and speaking. The student wrote: "I came into the class expecting to gnaw my arm off at the elbow and was pleased I didn't have to do that." Hey, that's high praise! He didn't have to resort to self-cannibalism!

But the principle is this. Everyone—and I mean EVERYONE—has been to a boring or plain bad meeting, keynote, conference presentation, or interview. If you're leading one of these events, you are guilty by association. And this is not like the justice system. Here you are guilty until proven innocent.

Which means that right up front, right after you've gotten their attention, you should give them some sort of motivation to sit and listen to you for the next however many minutes.

This is usually done by painting a picture of what could be.

REMOVE OBSTACLES

There are always barriers to getting your audience's attention. But you will probably not ever know what they are. They could be awaiting a doctor's phone call about a deadly diagnosis, they might have been up all night with a newborn baby, they might have a hot sales lead that has captured their heart, or they may hate the topic— or even hate you!

As much as we are able as a presenter, we should ease the mind of the audience.

At the onset of a workshop Alan was teaching, the class was notice-ably antsy. All of them had their phones out. At one point Alan noted that no one was even looking at him. He stopped them cold. "What is going on? None of you are mentally here." The leader sheepishly confessed, "We're waiting on the annual report today. All of our retirement dates will probably change today." Oh, so THAT was what it was. It wasn't boredom. There was a bigger fish on the other line.

He said, "Hey, folks. I get it. Wish I had some of your stock. But I'm going to be judged and graded on how well we accomplish our tasks in the next few hours. Can we agree that looking at your phones will not change the news you're about to get? (They all nodded.)

Then I ask you to put down the phones, and we'll check them at break. I promise it'll be less than an hour. If it's good news, I'll lead the conga line. If it's bad news, drinks are on me after work. But let's focus." And with that, he had relieved their biggest issue. All but one left their phones down completely until the break, and the good news they received was made even better by the anticipation.

In another setting, a divisional VP was fired and replaced by someone way down the org chart. Usually there is a succession order and this new VP was not in the line. (Think third son's adopted child's spouse being crowned King of England). The new VP called for a Town Hall meeting to address the troops. Everyone had the same thing on their mind: How'd YOU get the job?! He opened with "I guess you're all wondering how I got this job. I thought we could spend a few moments addressing that before we talk shop." Heads bobbed. A few people sheepishly cut eyes with their friends. He invited the CEO (his boss) to the stage. They chatted for a few minutes about the challenge before them, the CEO gave a little soliloquy about his thought process, and the challenge was issued. "This guy has some great ideas. We'll all be better if we listen to them. Get to it!" and the meeting *really* started. Had the VP failed to address the central question, he likely would have lost a lot of good will and had enemies before the end of his first meeting.

Here are some things you may need to address (if they apply) to remove the obstacle in your audience's minds:

- Your credentials (if they don't know you; don't cover this if they do!)

- How you'll take questions

- When breaks will occur

- How lunch and/or dismissal will occur

- Where they can get additional information

- 800-pound gorillas in the room
- Pink elephants (and silver goldfish)
- How to manage the materials/notes
- Backdrop of why you are presenting

Next, we'll look at delivering the main message of your presentation.

CHAPTER 20

EDUCATING

"Speeches that are measured by the hour will die with the hour."

— Thomas Jefferson

Most of the time you're presenting, the action or result you want happens after you present. If you're pitching a big project, they likely won't decide when you're in the room. They're accepting other bids, then the decision-makers will go into a room by themselves and decide. You won't be there. If you're giving great technological tips at a conference, they won't use them until they're back at their office several days later. At a team meeting, there are lots of ideas thrown out. But your staff won't use them until they're back at their desks.

The goal you have as a presenter then has to center around the audience keeping your content in mind until later. This adage applies 100 percent of the time: YOUR AUDIENCE CAN'T REPEAT WHAT THEY DON'T REMEMBER.

Your content needs to be memorable and useful to someone at a later date. In order to make your content more memorable, there are three tactics and strategies to consider:

FIND YOUR ONE SENTENCE

If you know what you'd like your audience to say when you're done, then your task is to package it in a way they can remember it. That usually means utilizing some sort of memory device (a rhyme, mnemonic, or powerful phrase). Remember the Gettysburg Address. It can't be long.

Martin Luther King Jr. turned on the power of repetition in his speech on August 28, 1963 on the Mall in Washington, D.C. It's become the title of one of the most famous speeches ever given on American soil. "I have a dream . . . " (He repeated it eight times during the speech.)

O.J. Simpson's murder trial turned on one simple, rhyming phrase from Johnny Cochran, "If the glove doesn't fit, you must acquit."

Barack Obama campaigned in 2008 on the single phrase "Hope and Change." Every voter in America (whether for or against President Obama) knew that phrase. We've yet to encounter a single person who can tell us what the Republican platform was that year.

Steve Jobs proclaimed in 2007, "It's a **widescreen iPod with touch controls**, a revolutionary **mobile phone** and a **breakthrough internet communications device**. Today, Apple is going to reinvent the phone." (OK, so the iPhone introduction was two sentences. We think we can still consider it a success.)

We know that memorizing material is hard. As a child we played the game Telephone. One person would quietly whisper a sentence to another. That person would whisper to the next. And on down the line. When the final message came out, it often had no resemblance to the original message. That's why it's so critical that we find a crisp message that is easy to repeat. We want people defending (and repeating) our views when we're not there.

A word of warning here. What people repeat is what they think you said. Once after a workshop, a student tweeted that Alan said content is unimportant. Of course Alan never said that. But if the student said he did, that's what was communicated. If after your talk a student says, "He was a complete bore," that's what you communicated, regardless of how well or how clearly you think you spoke.

PROVIDE A REPEATABLE STRUCTURE

Ever wonder why phone numbers aren't just seven (or ten) consecutive numbers? We put dashes or parentheses to break them up. 919-360-4702. Every time you quote a number (which is rare now), you say them in a little cadence with pauses at the dashes. It's a structure you're used to, and it works.

We learned the notes in sheet music from Acronyms: Every **G**ood **B**oy **D**oes **F**ine and FACE.

As a kid, Alan used to pour over the baseball box scores in the newspaper. He would look for things like home runs, game-winning RBIs, and lowest hit totals. It was easy to find those stats in seconds because the data was always in the same place/format. It had structure.

Structure gives the brain a place to put all that detail. We like to call your main structure points "buckets." Everyone knows what to do with buckets. You fill them up. But they can only hold a certain amount. That amount is dictated by time.

ASKING QUESTIONS

Most of us would love to have better answers from our audience during our presentations. But in order to get better answers, we need to ask better questions. Many presenters default to asking poor questions that get nothing but grunts. A great example in pop culture is in the movie *Ferris Bueller's Day Off*. Ben Stein plays an economics teacher who is dreadful at asking questions. In a monotone voice, he asks such beauties as "Anyone? Anyone?" "Raised or lowered? Raised? Did it work? Anyone know the effects?"

Nobody responds to these sorts of questions because it's obvious that the presenter doesn't want a response. It's even more shameful to make fun of the audience for not answering. That doesn't make them want to be more involved.

But you can get better answers by asking open-ended questions using a powerful word. We call it the Magic Word of Questions. What is the Magic Word of Questions, you ask? We agree. What is the magic word of questions. WHAT is the magic word of questions. Open your questions with what (or perhaps how) and you'll get much better responses. For example, if I ask my kids, "Did you have a good day today?" I'm likely to get a grunt, or more likely "I don't know." If I change that to "What was the best thing about your day?" or "What is something you'd like to have done differently today?" I'm a lot more likely to get a response, and maybe even a conversation. Unless they're a teenager. In that case, they've taken a sacred vow to never speak more than three words in a row to an adult.

There is a whole host of questions that presenters often use that fall into this domain of unuseful questions. Questions like, "Are there any questions? Are you with me? Does that make sense? Right?" Usually those are just habitual non-words that the speaker uses over and over. It's distracting and does nothing to engage the audience. Practice creating and asking useful questions and you'll get rewarded with not only an engaged audience but answers that help you make decisions and drive a sales process forward.

Now let's figure out how to close your presentation.

CHAPTER 21

REQUESTING

"ABC. 'A', always. 'B', be. 'C', closing.
ALWAYS BE CLOSING. Always be closing."

— Blake
(Alec Baldwin character in *Glengarry Glen Ross*)

Perhaps the hardest part about giving a presentation is finishing. Presenters often start out wondering how they'll ever speak for 50 minutes (or three hours) and by the time they get halfway through their allotted time on stage, they have no idea how they'll ever get through all their material. The finish line is determined by your objectives; the detail you go into is determined by your allotted time. And you WILL finish on time!

Now, assuming you've covered everything that has to be covered, how do you gracefully end your presentation?

WE CAN'T FINISH WHAT NEVER ENDS

At some point, the audience needs to leave. They're not coming to live with you after all. Too often, audiences walk out when a presentation runs over. "I've got a 2 p.m, sorry, need to run." But even more sad is when an audience stays until the end and leaves with nothing of value.

Here are three things that need to be covered as you wrap up. This entire part should be a fraction of your time on stage. Aim for five percent or less of your total time.

REPEAT THE ESSENTIAL (SUMMARIZE)

We've reminded you several times that your audience is not going to remember and repeat everything you've said. That's probably true for any message with more than one sentence. As you think about winding up your talk, consider what you'd like your audience to say if they were asked, "Hey, what'd you learn in that talk you went to?" You don't want to sound like a bore. So what should they repeat?

That's back to what we worked on in chapters 11 and 12. Your essential message. And as you take the exit ramp to the close, it's time to make key points clear. Some people call it a summary. Some people might refer to it as a recap. It doesn't matter what you call it. Systematically, it needs to complete the idea, "If you don't remember anything else we covered today, remember . . ." This is also something you can do by section. Usually it's on the level of your main structure. In this section of the book, we're wanting you to remember S.I.L.V.E.R. In Section II, it was five by five (Loud and Clear). We'll summarize in chapter 24 what we think you should remember about the whole book.

It could sound like this:

- As you consider your buying options for ___, it's key to remember . . .

- As we've examined the technique of fourth order non-linear time series analysis using Nyquist diagrams to show convergence in the frequency domain, the three things to consider are . . .

- We've looked at the forecast and the history of our spending as we transition to the new fiscal year. As you go back to your office, please remember . . .

A few reminders about closing clarity:

- It's one (maybe two sentences). This is not the place to tell a story or offer an additional opinion or add detail. 1. 2. 3. Done.

- No subtlety—be direct and clear. Don't imply. Lay it out there.

- This is a time to exhibit passion and energy. Don't limp to the finish. Go big!

ASK FOR YOUR OUTCOMES (OBJECTIVES)

To get what you want, all you have to do is ask for it. Well, we know that's not true. Alan's daughter has asked for a puppy every year since she was a toddler, and she's still waiting for the delivery of the dog. Asking is usually necessary, but it's not sufficient.

Circling back to your objective, what do you want to accomplish as a result of your presentation? And how do you plan to obtain that? This is the power of The Ask, often tucked conveniently into the close of your talk.

Much of the technique in asking is tied up in culture. Do you just outright ask for their signature? The promotion? Their commitment? Or should you subtly imply that it's a good idea or that you'd be pleased with the opportunity? Should it be bolted on the back end with no warning or segue? Or should you lay it out in the open up front and then come back to it as you close?

All of those answers come from your audience and what has led to you being on the stage in the first place. Let's look at an example of making a difficult ask.

In May 1961, President Kennedy was giving a speech to Congress asking for approval of his budget. He was including a rather large line item for the space program. History has been kind to JFK with regard to the space program—the United States launches many of their rockets from a facility named in his honor. But at the time of this speech, space exploration was considered a boondoggle by most of America. There were other issues deemed a lot more important: civil rights, the Cold War, poverty. And the track record for space launches was hardly good news. In 1960, only 16 of 37 launches were successful. Many of the rest ended in spectacular, flaming failure. And here was the president, asking for money. Look at the text as he transitioned to the ask:

> I therefore ask the Congress, above and beyond the increases I have earlier requested for space activities, to provide the funds which are needed to meet the following national goals:

> First, I believe that this nation should commit itself to achieving the goal, before this decade is out, of landing a man on the moon and returning him safely to the earth. No single space project in this period will be more impressive to mankind, or more important for the long-range exploration of space; and none will be so difficult or expensive to accomplish.

He asked for money. In his speech he went on to name amounts and what they would go toward. But he also made an appeal to his belief, and he outlined the benefits and consequences. It wasn't all rosy. He clearly gave the grim reality of the costs involved, both in dollars and manpower (and eventually, astronaut lives).

This is the prototypical ask. We call it the CAR. Claim. Action. Result.

> Claim: belief the nation should go to the moon

> Ask: approve the money (even above and beyond the previous amounts)

> Result: nothing more impressive, more important to space exploration (and difficult and expensive)

President Kennedy got his money. The US frantically edged ahead in the space race. And on July 20, 1969, with one-fifth of the world watching on live TV, Neil Armstrong planted his footprint in the soft dust of the moon.

You can use CAR statements to structure your ask. With a little practice, you'll find they roll right off your tongue.

> I've found that . . . I'd ask you to . . . You'll find . . .

> In my opinion . . . Would you please . . . As a result . . .

> I believe . . . Your mission, should you choose to accept it . . . The benefits will be . . .

By laying out a personal stake in the action and giving concrete results (even admitting the costs), you join the audience in addressing and deciding whatever you've come to obtain.

CLOSE FULL CIRCLE

The principle for your last words is "end like you started."

The following table shows how this might look:

If you started with	Then consider ending with . . .
. . . a story (or part of a story)	. . . the rest of the story or a connection to the story
. . . humor	. . . humor or the opposite, serious side to the humor
. . . an analogy	. . . connecting the analogy
. . . quote or reference	. . . another quote or a revisit to the concept
. . . picture or prop	. . . another picture or revisit the original picture
. . . current event	. . . a revisit to the event or predict the future
. . . a question	. . . the answer

Remember that your open (and by inference) your close are just entry (and exit) points to your topic. Don't use a random story that has nothing to do with your topic. End strong, on your terms.

Do not end with "That's all I've got" or "I guess that sums it up"! When you're done, be done. Craft your mic drop closing phrase and walk off the stage.

CHAPTER 22

SILVER PRESENTATION MATRIX

HOW TO USE THIS MATRIX:

During each step of the creation process, advance through the skills to make your presentation Loud and Clear.

P R E P A R A T I O N

		STARTING	ILLUSTRATING	LEARNING
I N T E R F E R E N C E	**1**	**COPY LAST PRESENTATION**	**CREATE A SLIDEUMENT**	**NO REHEARSAL OR PRACTICE**
	TIP	Start with your (or someone else's) last presentation. You change the date, the group, and a few other slides. Easy to produce, dangerous to present. **TIP:** Don't copy. Close PowerPoint and begin with a pen and paper and make an outline first.	You fear leaving something out, so you put it on the slide. Pretty soon you have a mammoth reference guide you're showing your audience. **TIP:** If you think your audience needs help after the presentation, design a separate handout.	Your schedule is packed. You know your stuff. Why practice? There are more important things to do (like those slides!) **TIP:** Schedule time to practice and rehearse your presentation, getting feedback from others.
D I S T O R T E D	**2**	**NO QUESTION OF WIIFY**	**USE TOO MUCH TEXT**	**RUN THROUGH SLIDES**
	TIP	Your presentation is about what you know, want, and feel. **TIP:** Ask "What's In It For You" from the audience point of view.	Guns don't kill presentations, bullets do. **TIP:** Use charts, pictures, and diagrams to effectively to communicate your key messages.	You run through the slides and have an inner monologue about what you'll say. You feel good. **TIP:** Simulate the exact environment you'll be presenting in. Practice out loud.
U N R E A D A B L E	**3**	**OBJECTIVES (NOT AGENDAS)**	**REPLACE TEXT WITH IMAGES/PROPS**	**PRACTICE OPENINGS/CLOSINGS**
	TIP	Every audience is different. **TIP:** Understand what your audience wants, what they need, and how they will best receive what you have to say.	It's a slide deck, not a slideument. **TIP:** Use strong images and limit the amount of text by avoiding readable sentences (short thoughts only).	An effective open captures the attention of the audience a strong close delivers the call to action. **TIP:** Practice your open and close at least twice as much as the main content.
R E A D A B L E	**4**	**USE STORIES & EXERCISES**	**HI-RES IMAGES & FEW BULLETS**	**REHEARSE AND VIDEOTAPE**
	TIP	We remember stories and we learn by doing. **TIP:** Start with a story that the audience can relate to. Give them an exercise that shows how the presentation relates to them personally.	Images are quicker and easier to digest and help memory recall **TIP:** Use hi-res images that you have permission to use and convey your message. Use the four power points to focus attention.	Good presenters rehearse until they get it right, great presenters rehearse until they never get it wrong. **TIP:** Mr. Canon doesn't lie. Video your practice and watch it to find what to correct.
C L E A R	**5**	**CREATE A MASTER METAPHOR**	**WORK WITH A DESIGNER**	**KNOW IT COLD**
	TIP	The goal is to create a memorable business presentation. **TIP:** Create a master metaphor that reinforces your messaging and ONE THING you want to communicate.	You can't see the label when you are inside the jar. Skills and an outside eye can help. **TIP:** Work with a graphic designer to maximize the impact and placement of your visuals.	Murphy's Law suggests that your presentation will rarely go the way you planned. **TIP:** Know your content so well that you can adjust if (when) things go wrong. A strong presenter doesn't miss a beat.

D E L I V E R Y

		VAULTING	**E**DUCATING	**R**EQUESTING
F **A** **D** **I** **N** **G**	**1**	**DRESS INAPPROPRIATELY**	**TRY TO COVER IT ALL**	**RUN OVER TIME ALLOTTED**
	TIP	You love your broken-in jeans and your style is retro-quaint. You don't much care what others think. **TIP:** Know your audience and dress to impress. Don't pile on by being an eyesore.	But you've got so much to share! And you try. **TIP:** Find the most important messages and find a creative way to make them stick.	It's easy to give excuses. The folks before you ran over. You had a lot to cover. People asked questions. There was a tech glitch. **TIP:** Honor your audience. End on time. No exceptions.
V **E** **R** **Y** **W** **E** **A** **K**	**2**	**INTRODUCING YOURSELF**	**LOPSIDE YOUR POINTS**	**THAT'S ALL I'VE GOT**
	TIP	It's easy to start with "a little about me." Either a) your audience already knows who you are, or b) they don't care. **TIP:** Get to something of interest from your very first word.	You spent 30 minutes on your first point, 10 on your second, and cover the remaining five in 5 minutes. **TIP:** Be mindful you can't cover everything you know. Balance your points and add detail in parallel to keep sections equal in size.	You speak until you run out of content. **TIP:** Start with an audience analysis. Find out who they are, what they want, what they need. Find custom connect points and invite them on the journey.
W **E** **A** **K**	**3**	**THANK EVERYONE**	**NO FLOW OR ORDER OF POINTS**	**END WITH Q&A**
	TIP	Southerners will chafe. But you were asked to give a presentation, not hand out accolades. **TIP:** Thank your audience at the end. And let that be your only "Thank You."	Random thoughts are good for brainstorms, but not for transfer of ideas. **TIP:** Have some sort of structure to your talk that audiences can follow. Let them know as you segue that progress is being made	Letting your audience end your presentation is asking for disaster. Usually it disintegrates until most have left (or wish they had). **TIP:** Take Q&A, save a fantastic finish that engages the entire audience.
G **O** **O** **D**	**4**	**SHARE INSIGHT AND WISDOM**	**RESET AUDIENCE EVERY 10 MINUTES**	**C2A (CALL TO ACTION)**
	TIP	If you only say things your audience already knows or could find out, what use are you to them? **TIP:** Explain the meaning and experience behind facts. Put numbers in context.	Just because you got your audience's attention doesn't mean you can keep it. Variety keeps things interesting. **TIP:** Strive to be different. Mix things up and reset your audience. Use exercises, questions or a video every ten minutes (or more!)	People respond (yes or no) to direct asked. But they have to be asked. **TIP:** Know what your audience needs. Ask for the sale; ask them to use the knowledge; ask them to change; ask them to take the opportunity.
L **O** **U** **D**	**5**	**OPEN WITH A STORY**	**USE A STICKY MEMORY DEVICE**	**CLOSING STORY & C2A**
	TIP	You don't get a second chance to make a strong first impression. **TIP:** Use an opening story rich in detail and drama to both capture attention and set the frame for your presentation.	A major goal of presenting is to be memorable. Catchy memory devices allow the audience to recall your message. **TIP:** Use an acronym, alliteration, or a saying to reinforce the main points from your presentation.	Want your message to stick, then be memorable at the end. **TIP:** End with your strongest story and be direct with what you want the audience to do. Give a clear call to action.

CHAPTER 23

SILVER PREPARATION GRID

SILVER PREPARATION GRID

S STARTING

TOPIC & OBJECTIVE	REASON TO LISTEN	"ONE THING"
DATE/TIME: TOPIC: OBJECTIVE:	WHAT WILL YOUR AUDIENCE GET FROM LISTENING TO YOU?	WHAT'S THE CENTRAL IDEA FOR THE AUDIENCE TO REMEMBER?

I ILLUSTRATING

OPENING	KEY POINTS	CLOSING / CALL TO ACTION
HOW WILL YOU OPEN? STORY, FACT, OR CURRENT EVENT?	#1 #2 #3	HOW WILL YOU CLOSE? WHAT DO YOU WANT THE AUDIENCE TO DO?

L LEARNING

NOTES / OUTLINE	PRACTICING	REHEARSING
REVIEW SLIDES AND DEVELOP NOTES. CREATE AN OUTLINE OF THE TALK DATE: TIME:	SCHEDULE TIME TO PRACTICE THE OPENING AND CLOSING PARTS OF YOUR TALK DATE: TIME:	SCHEDULE TIME TO REHEARSE FROM BEGINNING TO END MULTIPLE TIMES DATE: TIME:

V VAULTING

INTRODUCTION	DRESS	OPENING
WHO IS INTRODUCING YOU AND WHAT ARE THEY SAYING? WHO: WHAT:	CONSIDER AUDIENCE, BACKDROP, AND FILMING CONSIDERATIONS:	FIRST WORDS COUNT. YOUR FIRST SIX WORDS ARE:

E EDUCATING

KEY POINT #1		KEY POINT #2		KEY POINT #3
INSIGHT: STORY: EXERCISE:	R E S E T A U D I E N C E	INSIGHT: STORY: EXERCISE:	R E S E T A U D I E N C E	INSIGHT: STORY: EXERCISE:

R REQUESTING

Q & C	CLOSING STORY	CALL TO ACTION
HOW WILL YOU HANDLE QUESTIONS & COMMENTS?	CLOSE WITH A STORY THAT TIES THE MAIN POINTS TOGETHER	THE FIRST SIX WORDS OF YOUR LAST SENTENCE ARE:

© 2020 STAN PHELPS AND ALAN HOFFLER

DOWNLOAD A COPY OF THIS GRID AT: https://www.millswyck.com/silvergoldfishresources/

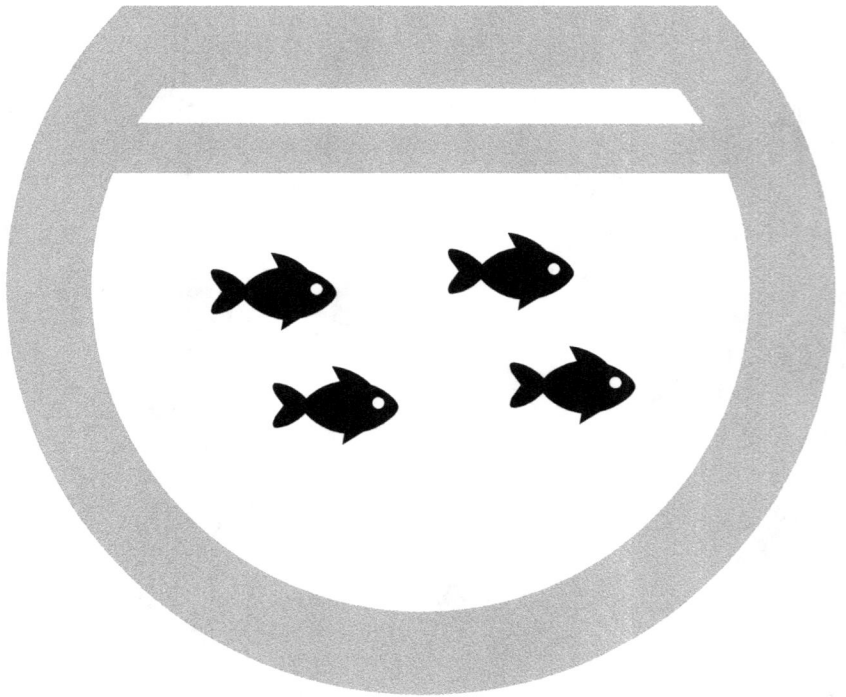

FINAL THOUGHTS

CHAPTER 24

FIVE TAKEAWAYS

"Life is a succession of lessons which must be lived to be understood. All is riddle, and the key to a riddle is another riddle."

— Ralph Waldo Emerson

H ere are our top five takeaways from *Silver Goldfish*:

1. THERE IS NO SILVER BULLET

   The only way we've found to get good at presenting is to work at it. If there were a pill, we'd sell you that instead.

2. NO ONE IS BORN A GREAT PRESENTER

   No one reading this book was born speaking. Not one of us. And we certainly weren't born speaking well. It's a skill, not a talent.

3. YOU NEED TO BE BOTH LOUD AND CLEAR

   Your audience has plenty to occupy their minds; you need to be louder. Your audience won't retain nearly as much as you think they should; you need to be clearer.

4. IT'S NOT ABOUT YOU THE PRESENTER

   Don't let your I's get too close together. Make your message about your audience.

5. BE REMEMBER-ABLE

   Success in presenting is that the audience can repeat your message. That's a tall order with so much information swirling in our lives. Find a way to help them remember your message.

Thank you for reading this book. Here's how you can help us improve business presentations by creating more Silver Goldfish thinkers:

- apply what you've learned in this book to nail your next presentation
- share the book with others
- bring us in to speak at your conference
- book us for a workshop or training session
- connect with us on LinkedIn

ABOUT THE AUTHORS

STAN PHELPS

Stan Phelps is a best-selling author, keynote speaker, and workshop facilitator. He believes that today's organizations must focus on meaningful differentiation to win the hearts of both employees and customers.

He is the founder of PurpleGoldfish.com. Purple Goldfish is a think tank of customer experience and employee engagement experts that offers keynotes and workshops that drive loyalty and sales. The group helps organizations connect with the hearts and minds of customers and employees.

Prior to PurpleGoldfish.com, Stan had a 20-year career in marketing that included leadership positions at IMG, adidas, PGA Exhibitions, and Synergy. At Synergy, he worked on award-winning experiential programs for top brands such as KFC, Wachovia, NASCAR, Starbucks, and M&M's.

Stan is a TEDx speaker, a Forbes contributor, and an IBM Futurist. His writing is syndicated on top sites such as Customer Think and Business2Community. He has spoken at more than 400 events across Australia, Bahrain, Canada, Ecuador, France, Germany, Holland, Israel, Japan, Malaysia, Peru, Russia, Singapore, Spain, Sweden, UK, and the US.

He is the author of 12 other business books:

- *Purple Goldfish 2.0 - 10 Ways to Attract Raving Customers*
- *Green Goldfish 2.0 - 15 Keys to Driving Employee Engagement*
- *Golden Goldfish - The Vital Few*
- *Blue Goldfish - Using Technology, Data, and Analytics to Drive Both Profits and Prophets*
- *Purple Goldfish Service Edition - 12 Ways Hotels, Restaurants, and Airlines Win the Right Customers*
- *Red Goldfish - Motivating Sales and Loyalty Through Shared Passion and Purpose*
- *Pink Goldfish - Defy Normal, Exploit Imperfection, and Captivate Your Customers*
- *Purple Goldfish Franchise Edition - The Ultimate S.Y.S.T.E.M. for Franchisors and Franchisees*
- *Yellow Goldfish - Nine Ways to Drive Happiness in Business for Growth, Productivity, and Prosperity*
- *Gray Goldfish - Navigating the Gray Areas to Successfully Lead Every Generation*
- *Red Goldfish Nonprofit Edition - How the Best Nonprofits Leverage Their Purpose to Increase Engagement and Impact*
- *Diamond Goldfish - Excel Under Pressure & Thrive in the Game of Business*

and one fun one...

- *Bar Tricks, Bad Jokes, & Even Worse Stories*

Stan received a BS in Marketing and Human Resources from Marist College, a JD/MBA from Villanova University, and a certificate for Achieving Breakthrough Service from Harvard Business School.

He is a Certified Net Promoter Associate, an instructor at the ANA School of Marketing, and has taught as an adjunct professor at NYU, Rutgers University, and Manhattanville College.

Stan is also a fellow at Maddock Douglas, an innovation consulting firm in Chicago. Stan lives in Cary, North Carolina, with his wife, Jennifer, and their two boys, Thomas and James.

To book Stan for an upcoming keynote, webinar, virtual talk, or workshop go to stanphelpsspeaks.com.

You can reach Stan at: stan@purplegoldfish.com, call +1.919.360.4702, or follow him on Twitter: @StanPhelpsPG.

ALAN HOFFLER

Alan Hoffler has an engineer's mind, a teacher's heart, and a coach's passion. His core belief is that great communication has the power to change a person, an organization, and the world.

He is the founder and executive director of MillsWyck Communications, leading the development of methods to train and coach people and organizations to excel in any environment where someone is speaking. He travels the world preparing groups for high-stakes presentations and inspiring groups to take an honest look at what they are saying—in every context. Some of his clients are changing the world through preserving natural resources in the Philippines, character education in Egypt, medical device sales across Europe, scaling agriculture and power in Africa, creating safe swimming environments, changing people's eating habits and exercise, speaking on the TEDx stage, and governing cities, counties, and states— and even leading families through better conversations with teenagers. He has coached speakers for college graduations, scholarship and job interviews, TEDx, Shark Tank, Toastmaster competitions, church education, and pitches ranging from fifty to fifty million dollars. He has been the fundraising emcee and keynote for events raising as much as $250,000 in a single night.

Alan is also the director of training for 3D Institute, a group devoted to changing the culture in sports around the world and an adjunct instructor at NC State University and the University of Richmond. Prior to his work as a speaker and speaking coach, he was a corporate trainer at SAS Institute, a software tester, a college calculus instructor, and a high school teacher and basketball coach. He presented nationally as a safety presenter for the Aviation Safety Foundation (now the Air Safety Institute).

Alan has degrees in Aerospace Engineering (BS) and Applied Mathematics (MS) from NC State University, owns a commercial pilot's license, and earned credentials as a certified 3D Coach presenter and certified SAS Presenter.

He is the author of *Presentation Sin,* his first book on speaking with excellence, and co-author of *6 Steps Forward,* a parable about navigating the stages in a man's life. He has been published in *Plane & Pilot* magazine and is an avid blogger.

Alan lives in Apex, North Carolina, with his wife Haley and their two almost-adults, Joel and Allyson. He actively enjoys sports photography, gardening, disc golf, and college football.

To book Alan for an upcoming keynote, webinar, or workshop go millswyck.com or alanhoffler.com. You can reach Alan at:

- Email: alan@millswyck.com
- Phone: +1.919.386.9238
- Twitter: @AlanHoffler

ADDITIONAL INSPIRATION AND RECOMMENDED READING

PRESENTING

Atkinson, Cliff. *Beyond Bullet Points: Using Microsoft Office Power-Point 2007 to Create Presentations That Inform, Motivate, and Inspire.* Redmond, WA: Microsoft Press, 2007.

Decker, Bert. *You've Got to Be Believed to Be Heard, Updated Edition: The Complete Book of Speaking . . . in Business and in Life!.* New York: St. Martin's Press, 2008.

Duarte, Nancy. *Resonate: Present Visual Stories That Transform Audiences.* J. Wiley & Sons, 2010.

Fugere, Brian, Chelsea Hardaway, and Jon Warshawsky. *Why Business People Speak Like Idiots: A Bullfighter's Guide.* New York City: Free Press, 2005.

Heath, Chip, and Dan Heath. *Made to Stick: Why Some Ideas Survive and Others Die.* New York: Random House, 2007.

Hoffler, Alan. *Presentation Sin: The Practical Guide to Stop Offending (and Start Impressing) Your Audience.* Cary, NC: CreateSpace, 2015.

Humes, James C. *Speak Like Churchill, Stand Like Lincoln: 21 Powerful Secrets of History's Greatest Speakers.* New York: Three Rivers Press, 2002.

Morgan, Nick. *Give Your Speech, Change the World: How to Move Your Audience to Action*. New York: Harvard Business School Press, 2005.

Stolovitch, Harold. *Telling Ain't Training*. Alexandria: ASTD, 2002.

Weissman, Jerry. *Presenting to Win: The Art of Telling Your Story*. Alexandria, VA: Prentice Hall, 2006.

VISUALS

Duarte, Nancy. *slide:ology: The Art and Science of Creating Great Presentations*. Sebastopol: O'Reilly Media, Inc., 2008.

Kosslyn, Stephen M. *Clear and to the Point: 8 Psychological Principles for Compelling PowerPoint Presentations*. New York: Oxford University Press, USA, 2007.

Medina, John. *Brain Rules: 12 Principles for Surviving and Thriving at Work, Home, and School* (Book & DVD). Chicago: Pear Press, 2008.

Reynolds, Garr. *Presentation Zen: Simple Ideas on Presentation Design and Delivery (Voices That Matter)*. Berkeley, CA: New Riders Press, 2008.

Roam, Dan. *The Back of the Napkin: Solving Problems and Selling Ideas with Pictures*. Ottawa: Portfolio Hardcover, 2008.

OTHER COLORS IN THE GOLDFISH SERIES

PURPLE GOLDFISH 2.0 – 10 WAYS TO ATTRACT RAVING CUSTOMERS

Purple Goldfish is based on the Purple Goldfish Project, a crowd-sourcing effort that collected more than 1,001 examples of signature-added value. The book draws inspiration from the concept of lagniappe, providing 10 practical strategies for winning the hearts of customers and influencing positive word of mouth.

GREEN GOLDFISH 2.0 – 15 KEYS TO DRIVING EMPLOYEE ENGAGEMENT

Green Goldfish is based on the simple premise that happy engaged employees create happy enthused customers. The book focuses on 15 different ways to drive employee engagement and reinforce a strong corporate culture.

GOLDEN GOLDFISH – THE VITAL FEW

Golden Goldfish examines the importance of your top 20 percent of customers and employees. The book showcases nine ways to drive loyalty and retention with these two critical groups.

BLUE GOLDFISH - USING TECHNOLOGY, DATA, AND ANALYTICS TO DRIVE BOTH PROFITS AND PROPHETS

Blue Goldfish examines how to leverage technology, data, and analytics to do a "little something extra" to improve the experience for the customer. The book is based on a collection of over 300 case studies. It examines the three R's: Relationship, Responsiveness, and Readiness. *Blue Goldfish* uncovers eight different ways to turn insights into action.

RED GOLDFISH - MOTIVATING SALES AND LOYALTY THROUGH SHARED PASSION AND PURPOSE

Purpose is changing the way we work and how customers choose business partners. It is driving loyalty, and it's on its way to becoming the ultimate differentiator in business. *Red Goldfish* shares cutting edge examples and reveals the eight ways businesses can embrace purpose that drives employee engagement, fuels the bottom line, and makes an impact on the lives of those it serves.

PURPLE GOLDFISH SERVICE EDITION - 12 WAYS HOTELS, RESTAURANTS, AND AIRLINES WIN THE RIGHT CUSTOMERS

Purple Goldfish Service Edition is about differentiation via added value and marketing to your existing customers via G.L.U.E. (giving little unexpected extras). Packed with over 100 examples, the book focuses on the 12 ways to do the "little extras" to improve the customer experience for restaurants, hotels, and airlines. The end result is increased sales, happier customers, and positive word of mouth.

PINK GOLDFISH - DEFY NORMAL, EXPLOIT IMPERFECTION, AND CAPTIVATE YOUR CUSTOMERS

Companies need to stand out in a crowded marketplace, but true differentiation is increasingly rare. Based on over 200 case studies, *Pink Goldfish* provides an unconventional seven-part framework for achieving competitive separation by embracing flaws instead of fixing them.

PURPLE GOLDFISH FRANCHISE EDITION - THE ULTIMATE S.Y.S.T.E.M. FOR FRANCHISORS AND FRANCHISEES

Packed with over 100 best-practice examples, *Purple Goldfish Franchise Edition* focuses on the six keys to creating a successful franchise S.Y.S.T.E.M. and a dozen ways to create a signature customer experience.

YELLOW GOLDFISH - NINE WAYS TO DRIVE HAPPINESS IN BUSINESS FOR GROWTH, PRODUCTIVITY, AND PROSPERITY

There should only be one success metric in business and that's happiness. A Yellow Goldfish is any time a business does a little extra to contribute to the happiness of its customers, employees, or society. Based on nearly 300 case studies, *Yellow Goldfish* provides a nine-part framework for happiness-driven growth, productivity, and prosperity in business.

GRAY GOLDFISH - NAVIGATING THE GRAY AREAS TO SUCCESSFULLY LEAD EVERY GENERATION

How do you successfully lead the five generations in today's workforce? You need tools to navigate. Filled with over 100 case studies and the Generational Matrix, *Gray Goldfish* provides the definitive map for leaders to follow as they recruit, train, manage, and inspire across the generations.

RED GOLDFISH NONPROFIT EDITION - HOW THE BEST NONPROFITS LEVERAGE THEIR PURPOSE TO INCREASE ENGAGEMENT AND IMPACT

The competition is fierce in the nonprofit world, even when competing in different spaces. This book explores the signature ways nonprofits reinforce their purpose and stand out in a crowded marketplace, whether it is an extra level of recognition for key donors, a special incentive designed to keep their best employees, or something simple like a luncheon to recognize volunteers or highest fundraisers. If you work at a nonprofit, this book will help you deliver "a little extra" to your stakeholders.

DIAMOND GOLDFISH - EXCEL UNDER PRESSURE & THRIVE IN THE GAME OF BUSINESS

Diamond Goldfish uncovers how business is a game. It's a guide for driving sales and deepening client relationships. Based on the Diamond Rule, over 150 case studies, and the science-backed framework of Market Force, the book provides perspective and tools for winning in sales and client management.

www.ingramcontent.com/pod-product-compliance
Lightning Source LLC
Chambersburg PA
CBHW071235290326
41931CB00038B/3032